PAPER PEONY PRE.

BRAVE
AND
BELOVED

AN IN-DEPTH STUDY OF WOMEN OF THE BIBLE

MEREDITH STORRS

For bulk, special sales, or ministry purchases, email: reagan@paperpeonypress.com

Author photo © Leslie Kosier

Cover, interior design, and illustrations by Jacy Corral

Brave and Beloved: An In-Depth Study of Women of the Bible
Copyright © 2022 Meredith Storrs
Published by Paper Peony Press
San Antonio, TX
www.paperpeonypress.com

ISBN 978-1-952842-83-2 (pbk)

Printed in China.

Contents

For Eloïse:
Oh how I long to show you
All About Brave Women

Before you begin, please scan this code for an intro message from Meredith.

PLUS A FREE BONUS!

Welcome!

I'm excited to take a walk with you into the world of women in the Bible. Understanding these spiritual ancestors of ours has been my nerdy obsession for more than a decade. I started by reading a number of popular books about women in the Bible, then flipping to the index of my favorites to find their source material. I read, and then read some more. I never plan to stop. Over time, this approach helped me to make sense of the stories that used to leave me scratching my head. I started to recognize when frustration or horror were actually the appropriate response to the injustices in a story. I was also humbled to learn that many of my childhood heroines had a dark side, and yet God still welcomed and loved them anyway.

The women in the Bible might not look, eat, shop, or speak like we do, but their stories are still incredibly relevant today. God uses women from all walks of life to accomplish his work in the world. By studying the diverse women in the Bible, we will see that God's design for womanhood is not one-size-fits-all. These women can inspire us to live godly lives—no matter our background, location, or personality—and teach us to trust in God's goodness wherever our road leads.

> *God's design for womanhood is not one-size-fits-all.*

Whether you have studied Hebrew or barely cracked a Bible before, this book is for you. As we read stories of key women in Scripture, I hope that you will hear God speaking through his Word, sharing more than simple morals or life advice. God invites us into his presence, constantly upending ancient cultural expectations and our own. And there, near to his heart, we will find the redemption and restoration that can finally set us free.

Your sister,

Meredith

How to Use This Study

A Note for Study Leaders

This study is divided into four parts with five lessons each, allowing you the flexibility to set your own pace, although I would encourage moving through no more than one or two lessons per week. The reading and study questions for each lesson are designed for prayerful introspection and should take an hour or more to complete. If discussion time is limited, I have bolded key questions in each lesson that you could prioritize.

I have intentionally omitted a teaching component for this study so that your discussion can focus on observations and personal reflections from members in your group. In most cases, there is no "right answer" to the questions, although some observations may veer away from either the passage itself or larger biblical principles. In those cases, it may be most helpful to guide the group back to the passage (or reference other sections of Scripture) that add clarity. As the group leader, you should feel empowered to add additional, context-specific reflection questions and/or teaching to help the content connect personally to those in your study group.

This book is made for consumption. Every lesson includes a passage from the Bible printed out for easy reference, with space to highlight, doodle, and take notes. There's a lot here to discover and ponder on your own, but it's even more fun with friends. Invite a few people to study with you and enjoy the wisdom and insight of differing perspectives.

In each lesson, you will...

Learn

Character Portraits introduce each woman.

Study Tools grow your ability to observe the details and analyze each story:

Meditation Literature	*What detail drives my imagination?*
Patterns	*What themes or repetition do I observe?*
Story Arrangement	*What does the biblical author say?*
Divine Authorship	*What does God reveal about himself?*
Character Speech	*What do the women say?*
A Broken World	*What needs redemption?*
Application	*How might this story impact my week?*

Read

Relevant passages of *Scripture* are printed within the book.

Cultural Notes and *Illustrations* give you context and explain key details.

Reflect

Study Questions guide your understanding of the passage and help you find ways to apply what you are learning.

Pray

Suggested *Prayer* prompts encourage meditation and response.

What's next?

Before we dive in, I want to share a little bit about the culture in which the Bible was written. This introduction will serve as a reference point throughout our study to help us understand the kinds of challenges biblical women faced and how God values women, even when others cannot see their worth.

Introduction: A Cultural Primer

I still remember the feeling I had sitting in Ritchie Spencer's Costume Design course my freshman year of college. It was an 8 a.m. class, but I always sat wide-eyed in the frontmost chair, scrawling copious notes to the dry monotone lectures that regularly put my fellow costume designers to sleep. I was never much of a history buff, but somehow, mentally donning the attire of Elizabethan England or ancient Egypt awakened my interest in all those important dates and wars and inventions. I could finally walk around in their shoes, now that I understood how they were designed and why.

As a student of the Bible, I experienced a similar renaissance when I began to learn more about the lives of women in the ancient world. While reading Scripture, we might picture a woman in a hijab, not yoga pants or a business suit, but the cultural difference between us runs much deeper than clothing and can significantly impact the way that we understand the Bible. Even though Scripture spans several thousand years, certain distinguishing realities separate our 21st century Western habits from theirs. Understanding these differences can provide clarity when a story's details prick our modern sensibilities. But more importantly, we should take note when details in the story deviate from the typical cultural script.

Is the culture of the Bible showing us the best way to live?

The Bible was written during a specific time span in a handful of locations in the ancient Near East. Understanding the cultural context of the passage you are reading will help the story make more sense, but we must be careful not to assume that *how things are* in a particular story is *how they should be*. Reading closely, we can learn when God's plan for humanity differs from the events and values of the day. Both then and now, God enters into our culture and works within broken systems to move us ever closer to the day when all things will be made new, just as perfect as they were in the Garden of Eden.

What was life like for women in biblical times?

Look for these numbered icons throughout our study:

Most people lived in small villages and shared households.

During the Iron Age (roughly Exodus through the end of the Israelite monarchy), most people in the Bible lived in small agricultural villages made up of several families from the same clan. Physical structures housed members of an extended family, and women moved into their husband's household once they were wed. Community was a natural feature of the home, where the patriarch might also house a younger brother's family and a widowed aunt or grandmother, in addition to his own family. The women shared chores and looked after each other's children. With the exception of pilgrimages for holy rituals, a woman would find very little reason to leave her home. Her own siblings might live in a household only a few miles away, but she could go years without seeing them. Even in Jesus' day, eighty to ninety percent of Israelites still lived in these smaller clan-based villages. Those in cities had homes with similar multi-generational family structures, although their lives would take them out into the marketplace more often.

Marriage was a social expectation,* not a preference.

Arranged by a woman's father with input from the older women in the family, marriage provided the needed social and financial support for a young woman. Marriages were ideally arranged within the clan but to a man from another household. While consent might be requested of a young girl, it was not required. The bride's dowry was given to her husband to manage but acted as financial security that the woman would receive back if he died or divorced her. During the Greek and Roman eras, marriages among the elite served to preserve wealth and social status, whereas men in lower classes would be more interested in finding a suitable helper for their line of work. A farmer would benefit from marrying the daughter of another farmer, just as a merchant would benefit from marrying a girl experienced on the loom.

Our modern idea of a "love match" in marriage is a fairly recent construct. While love in marriage was highly praised, as we see in Song of Songs, marriage arrangements in biblical times were primarily economic. Women and children were viewed as such a valuable asset that they would be counted among a man's personal wealth. Like Eve before her, a good wife was a valuable partner to support the work of her family—she was essential for both procreation as well as economic viability. A good wife was, quite literally, more precious than jewels.[1]

For the purpose of this summary, I am describing the experience of freeborn women in Israel but should note that enslaved women would neither share these social expectations, nor have any opportunity to pursue them.

Monogamy was the ideal.

In the Bible, we do see many examples of polygamy, especially among the patriarchs and kings. Men needed an heir for both family name and property, so if a wife was unable to have a baby, he might take a second wife or seek to have children through a concubine or slave in his household. When we look at these examples of polygamy in Scripture, consistent themes of rivalry and family discord emerge. Understandably, bringing a second wife into the household could be devastating to the first, who in some cases might be cruelly treated or even abandoned for offering nothing more than another mouth to feed. While Hebrew law formally protected women from mistreatment, the cultural reality of this oft-unfaithful people group underscored the fraught relationships and rivalries that developed among a man's wives. By the Roman era, it was common for men to simply divorce a barren wife because Greek and Roman society did not permit polygamy. Jews, who adopted this practice around the same time, were confronted by Jesus' teaching that divorce should only be permissible in cases of infidelity, not barrenness or preference.

Children were a woman's ultimate goal, honor, and blessing.

The Hebrew people eagerly followed the creation mandate to be fruitful and multiply[2] and viewed children as essential to agricultural success and to the preservation of lineage. Once a girl reached childbearing capacity, arrangements for her marriage would begin. In the Old Testament era, most girls married between the ages of 12–18 and were anywhere from eight to fifteen years younger than their husbands. In Jesus' day, women were typically still at least five years younger than their spouses. With an average life expectancy of about 40, a woman might birth four children and would consider herself lucky if two survived to adulthood. Some estimates suggest that a quarter of women would die in childbirth, so older women with many children—especially sons—would have a higher status in their village and be viewed as abundantly blessed by God. By contrast, a barren woman was afflicted by more than low status. Even if her husband did not cast her out, she risked abandonment later in life with no surviving children to care for her once her husband died.

Work centered around the home.

In agricultural societies, both men and women participated in the family business. Because women in the household were often either pregnant, nursing, or caring for young children, their work needed to be compatible with childcare. They focused on tasks near the house while men went into the field to sow or into town to sell. Unlike the separate spheres of workplace versus home popularized after the industrial revolution, labor was divided according to capacity, but men and women remained united in the same vocational goal. Labor in agricultural societies also included seasons of crossover, like harvest or wine production, when all available hands joined in. By age 12 or 13, children were expected to contribute a full workload.

In many homes, women's productive tasks included cooking, weaving fabric, pottery making, basket weaving, spinning, gardening, drawing water, and grinding grain. It was typical for a woman to nurse for two to three years before weaning and becoming pregnant again. Once her children were grown (assuming she hadn't died in childbirth), a woman might take on other professional roles like midwife, mourner, perfumer, or healer. If a woman was particularly skilled in weaving, pottery, or the like, she might be able to produce more than her family needed and sell the surplus in the market. In Exodus, we see God specifically assign women to spin the yarn and fine linen for the tabernacle—an honored job they would have done on top of their usual family responsibilities that benefitted the entire community.

By Jesus' day, women were an active presence in the economy, working alongside their husbands in their family vocation. Some wealthy Roman and Greek women were required to stay in the home at all times so that their husband could ensure their protection and faithfulness. Out of necessity, lower-class women had greater freedom to work in public, but their childcare priorities meant that daily activities needed to be close to home or somehow compatible with their children's needs. When Paul instructs women to be managing or working in the home,[3] we should infer this as a place of industry. Home was not the opposite of work, but the natural place where work was accomplished during this time period.

 ## Most education was vocational training.

Aside from rabbinical schools for boys, most children were not educated in a formal classroom. Children in agricultural societies began their training as early as they could carry a bundle or hold a hand spindle. Fathers were responsible for training sons to carry on the family business just as mothers prepared their daughters for the practical skills needed to care for their future home and family. Mothers were also in charge of the children's moral development, socialization, and cultural transmission. Paul credits Timothy's mother Eunice and grandmother Lois for instilling good values in him,[4] just as King Lemuel recognizes his mother for teaching him the values to look for in a wife.[5] Understanding the mother's role in cultural transmission also explains why it would be such a huge detriment to marry a foreign woman. Mixing ethnic groups is not the concern here. Instead, Israelites were to avoid the likelihood that a foreign mother would pass along her own culture and gods to the children instead of the values and history of God's people.

Greek schools focused on physical education, literature, and music, and the Romans added mathematics and rhetoric to the curriculum. In wealthy families, Roman girls were sometimes educated up to our equivalent of middle school but usually stopped their schooling once married. Families who needed to put bread on the table found little use for memorizing literature and the rhetoric of philosophers, so what we understand of the Greek and Roman education system would apply only to wealthier citizens. Other families would provide vocational training, similar to previous eras.

 ## Women worshiped within their home.

Nursing and periods of uncleanliness like menstruation and postpartum would have often prevented women from participating in pilgrimages to holy places for formal sacrifice and ritual. As a result, much personal worship happened in the home. The Bible is clear that God demands exclusive worship, and yet the Israelites rarely live up to this standard. Archeological evidence supports this lived reality, as small figurines are often littered throughout home excavations. With such a heavy emphasis on childbearing, women were especially tempted to pursue cultic practices surrounding fertility. They worshiped Isis, Astarte, or the Queen of Heaven in hopes of bearing a child. These statues represented not only the family worship, but also financial equity.

While the social pressures and cultural norms for women in the Bible may feel foreign to us today, understanding their context helps us to see the truly remarkable ways in which we are united to those who came before us. Like a performer whose posture and movement changes while wearing a corset and bustle, women in antiquity come to life in a new way when we dress them in context.

More importantly, understanding the world of women in the Bible helps us to see just how radical Jesus' interactions with women were.

In an era when men would rarely speak to their own wives in a public space, Jesus approaches the woman at the well.

Though men were permitted to divorce a wife for showing unbound hair in public, Jesus honors Mary for the incredibly intimate way she uses her own hair to anoint his feet with oil.

Men could discard their wives for any number of reasons, and yet Jesus speaks against divorce, upholding the spirit of protection that the Law was intended to provide for women.

Men viewed themselves as intellectuals, worthy to participate in discussion and debate, and associated women with the senses. But Jesus incorporates cultural analogies in his teaching that appeal to both men and women, inviting all people to listen and learn.

Jesus treats women as though Genesis were actually true, as though we really are equally made in the image of God. Our God becomes flesh, steps into a particular cultural moment, and regularly upsets the expectations of those around them.

He invites Mary of Bethany to sit at his feet to learn. He exhorts the women at the tomb to proclaim the good news of his resurrection. And he welcomes us too, if only we have ears to hear. •

PART ONE

The Matriarchs

listen
observe
enjoy

Eve

Character Portrait

Who	The mother of all living, made together with the first man to be God's representatives on Earth
When	The dawn of creation
Where	The Garden of Eden, a utopia where all of creation had direct access to the presence of God

Study Tool
Meditation Literature — *Getting Lost in the Story*

When we first pick up something to read, our brains make several automatic calculations. We read a letter from our child's school differently than a fairy tale, a recipe differently than the terms and conditions for our cell phone contract. Each of these texts has a different author and unique purpose, which adjusts our expectations for what we will find.

The same is true of the Bible. It is composed of several genres of writing by different authors throughout history, which will influence the way we understand each part. And while the Bible does include some "thou shalls" and "thou shalt nots," it is not primarily a rule book.

It is a story.

Each book, chapter, and different style of writing in the Bible contributes to a unified purpose. It is God's way of revealing himself to us. Instead of providing draft documents for a 3D model or an extended bullet-point resume, God chose to reveal himself through stories. In one sense, these stories are so approachable that a child can follow along. But they are also deeply profound and designed to reveal more about God the more that we study them. As meditation literature, Scripture constantly repeats thematic elements, plot structures, words, and phrases, inviting us to compare, contrast, and consider what God might be showing us about himself and our relationship to him. Over the course of a lifetime, by reading and re-reading and talking about these stories together, we will draw new connections between passages and discover a richer understanding of our world.[6]

The goal of this study is not exhaustive understanding. Even if we had space to dive deeply into each story, the Bible isn't a video game where you collect all the coins, find every Easter egg, and beat the boss to get to the next level. Instead of focusing on completing tasks, I encourage you to approach your reading more like quality time with a friend. The study questions are not homework boxes to check, but an invitation to meditate, to dwell. So listen. Observe. Enjoy. Take your time. God is sharing himself with you. And because we are made like him, learning about him is the best way to understand ourselves. ●

Lesson 1
Passage

Before time eternal, God existed. When he decided to create the world we know today, he built a beautiful place and populated it with flora, fauna, and two people made in his image: Adam and Eve.

A Broken Motherhood

The story of creation and humanity's first sin is steeped in mothering imagery, and while this does not mean that childbirth will be every woman's calling, it does establish a thematic element we will see repeated throughout the Bible.

Made in the image of God, men and women have significant similarities, but a particular distinction of woman is her ability to bear children. Together, humans are called to be fruitful and multiply, and the woman's body is the essential vessel to make that happen. No pregnancies, no children, and no lineage happen without the female body to house them. Sadly, what was designed in utopia as a great honor is now a source of deep pain. Not only will pregnancy require a significant burden on a woman's body in the best-case scenario, birth itself will be painful and for much of human history, quite deadly. Then, in the unique physical vulnerability of childbirth, the man who should have been her greatest ally will now regularly be a source of strife.[7]

As we continue through the Bible, we will see cycles of this curse repeated from story to story—men harming those women who should have been in their care and women experiencing great sorrow in barrenness, broken families, wayward children, maternal mortality, and more.

GENESIS 1:26-31

26 Then God said, "Let us make man in our image, according to our likeness. They will rule the fish of the sea, the birds of the sky, the livestock, the whole earth, and the creatures that crawl on the earth."

27 So God created man in his own image;
he created him in the image of God;
he created them male and female.

28 God blessed them, and God said to them, "Be fruitful, multiply, fill the earth, and subdue it. Rule the fish of the sea, the birds of the sky, and every creature that crawls on the earth." 29 God also said, "Look, I have given you every seed-bearing plant on the surface of the entire earth and every tree whose fruit contains seed. This will be food for you, 30 for all the wildlife of the earth, for every bird of the sky, and for every creature that crawls on the earth — everything having the breath of life in it — I have given every green plant for food." And it was so. 31 God saw all that he had made, and it was very good indeed. Evening came and then morning: the sixth day.

GENESIS 2:15-25

15 The LORD God took the man and placed him in the garden of Eden to work it and watch over it. 16 And the LORD God commanded the man, "You are free to eat from any tree of the garden, 17 but you must not eat from the tree of the knowledge of good and evil, for on the day you eat from it, you will certainly die." 18 Then the LORD God said, "It is not good for the man to be alone. I will make a helper corresponding to him." 19 The LORD God formed out of the ground every wild animal and every bird of the sky, and brought each to the man to see what he would call it. And whatever the man called a living creature, that was its name.

20 The man gave names to all the livestock, to the birds of the sky, and to every wild animal; but for the man no helper was found corresponding to him. 21 So the LORD God caused a deep sleep to come over the man, and he slept. God took one of his ribs and closed the flesh at that place. 22 Then the LORD God made the rib he had taken from the man into a woman and brought her to the man. 23 And the man said:

This one, at last, is bone of my bone
and flesh of my flesh;
this one will be called "woman,"
for she was taken from man.

24 This is why a man leaves his father and mother and bonds with his wife, and they become one flesh. 25 Both the man and his wife were naked, yet felt no shame.

GENESIS 3:1-3:19

THE TEMPTATION AND THE FALL

1 Now the serpent was the most cunning of all the wild animals that the LORD God had made. He said to the woman, "Did God really say, 'You can't eat from any tree in the garden'?"

2 The woman said to the serpent, "We may eat the fruit from the trees in the garden. 3 But about the fruit of the tree in the middle of the garden, God said, 'You must not eat it or touch it, or you will die.'"

4 "No! You will certainly not die," the serpent said to the woman. 5 "In fact, God knows that when you eat it your eyes will be opened and you will be like God, knowing good and evil." 6 The woman saw that the tree was good for food and delightful to look at, and that it was desirable for obtaining wisdom. So she took some of its fruit and ate it; she also gave some to her husband, who was with her, and he ate it. 7 Then the eyes of both of them were opened, and they knew they were naked; so they sewed fig leaves together and made coverings for themselves.

SIN'S CONSEQUENCES

8 Then the man and his wife heard the sound of the LORD God walking in the garden at the time of the evening breeze, and they hid from the LORD God among the trees of the garden. 9 So the LORD God called out to the man and said to him, "Where are you?"

10 And he said, "I heard you in the garden, and I was afraid because I was naked, so I hid."

11 Then he asked, "Who told you that you were naked? Did you eat from the tree that I commanded you not to eat from?"

12 The man replied, "The woman you gave to be with me — she gave me some fruit from the tree, and I ate."

13 So the LORD God asked the woman, "What have you done?"

And the woman said, "The serpent deceived me, and I ate."

14 So the LORD God said to the serpent:

> Because you have done this,
> you are cursed more than any livestock
> and more than any wild animal.

> You will move on your belly
> and eat dust all the days of your life.
> 15 I will put hostility between you and the woman,
> and between your offspring and her offspring.
> He will strike your head,
> and you will strike his heel.

16 He said to the woman:

> I will intensify your labor pains;
> you will bear children with painful effort.
> Your desire will be for your husband,
> yet he will rule over you.

17 And he said to the man, "Because you listened to your wife and ate from the tree about which I commanded you, 'Do not eat from it':

> The ground is cursed because of you.
> You will eat from it by means of painful labor
> all the days of your life.
> 18 It will produce thorns and thistles for you,
> and you will eat the plants of the field.
> 19 You will eat bread by the sweat of your brow
> until you return to the ground,
> since you were taken from it.
> For you are dust,
> and you will return to dust."

GENESIS 3:20-24

20 The man named his wife Eve because she was the mother of all the living. 21 The LORD God made clothing from skins for the man and his wife, and he clothed them.

22 The LORD God said, "Since the man has become like one of us, knowing good and evil, he must not reach out, take from the tree of life, eat, and live forever." 23 So the LORD God sent him away from the garden of Eden to work the ground from which he was taken. 24 He drove the man out and stationed the cherubim and the flaming, whirling sword east of the garden of Eden to guard the way to the tree of life.

Lesson 1 Questions

1. **What does God say about Eve before she and Adam sin? How are they described and what two jobs does God give them?**

2. How does God react to Adam and Eve's sin? In what tone of voice do you hear his reaction? What does his reaction teach us about how God views people?

3. Think about the ways that you react when someone violates a rule that you've made. How is this similar to or different from the way God reacts to Adam and Eve?

4. What do you notice about the aspects of Eve's life that are now cursed?

5. **Adam and Eve are designed as partners in the tasks that God has given them. How are they dependent on one another to accomplish their calling? How does each one's curse make this job more difficult for both of them?**

6. Draw a picture of how you imagine the phrase "mother of all living." What personal experiences or stories inform your picture?

7. Rather than draw near to God's presence for wisdom, Adam and Eve reach for a shortcut. They choose to do what is right in their own eyes instead of following God's direction. This temptation will be revisited in future stories and is one that we wrestle with today. Think about what you know (or have heard) about God. How much overlap do you find between what God tells us to do and what seems wise to you?

What God says is wise

What seems wise to me

8. The very first pages of the Bible present an incredible utopia, which is quickly tarnished and seemingly lost forever. In what ways do you feel the effects of this curse on humanity and the created world today?

Lesson 1
Prayer

When God curses the serpent, he gives Adam and Eve a glimmer of hope. Things will get pretty bad, but he has a plan for restoration that will one day come through Eve's childbearing. Write a prayer in response to this promise. What about God gives you reason to hope? What hopes do you have for restoration in your own life? What questions or fears do you want to confess?

New to the idea of prayer?

At its core, prayer is talking to God. The Bible contains God's message to us, and prayer is our opportunity to respond. Prayer doesn't have to sound holy or use fancy words. It can be raw and honest as we are wrestling through the difficult parts of life. It often becomes reverent and precious as we begin to understand all that this holy God has done for us and the wild notion that we could have access to such a good Father. So dive in—you can speak your prayers out loud, inside your head, or write them down here.

Sarah

Character Portrait

Who	The wife of Abraham and the mother of the nation of Israel
When	Middle Bronze Age, approximately 2000–1800 BC
Where	Ur, Egypt, and eventually Canaan

Study Tool

A Broken World — *Humans will be Human*

If you were introduced to Bible stories as a child, reading them again as an adult might raise a number of questions. Children's Bibles (thankfully) skip graphic details that are not developmentally appropriate, but sometimes in summarizing a particular story, the author makes the humans into heroes. As we consider the women in the Bible, we find many honored for their faithfulness and lifted up as role models. But people in the Bible are also flawed. The Bible is not a collection of Christian superheroes. It is God's story, designed to show us how he is the Hero of Heroes in a world that is hopelessly broken. Outside of the Garden of Eden, we should expect evil to flourish, even in the hearts of those God chooses to love. The Bible is not a record of how bad things happen to good people but of good that happens, despite a wicked world.[8]

As you read, look for clues that indicate whether a particular human action should be viewed as admirable or not. And when our good girls sometimes do bad things, watch how God intervenes, partnering with even imperfect women to do his perfect work. •

Lesson 2
Passage

After Adam and Eve are sent away from the garden, the story goes from bad to worse. God floods the world and starts again from scratch, but the curse of sin continues. So God begins a new chapter. He invites a different man and woman to be his representatives on earth. He appoints Abram and Sarai with a new home and new names—Abraham and Sarah—welcoming them into the calling to be fruitful with the promise of a family miracle.

God Sees Hagar

Hagar's sad and troubling story is one of many moments that reveal Sarah's sinful humanity. In one sense, we might understand Sarah's fear and frustration, given both the general social pressure of having children ❹ as well as God's promise to make Abram into a great nation. At the same time, she disregards Hagar's personhood, forcing her to bear a child for Abram, ❸ and then blames and punishes Hagar for the whole mess.

God does not ignore Hagar's suffering, though. He makes a separate covenant with Hagar and gives her the great honor of being the first person in Scripture to give a name to God: *El-roi*, "the one who sees me." You can read this part of the story by looking up Genesis 16:7–16 in your own Bible or online.

GENESIS 12:10-20

¹⁰ There was a famine in the land, so Abram went down to Egypt to stay there for a while because the famine in the land was severe. ¹¹ When he was about to enter Egypt, he said to his wife, Sarai, "Look, I know what a beautiful woman you are. ¹² When the Egyptians see you, they will say, 'This is his wife.' They will kill me but let you live. ¹³ Please say you're my sister so it will go well for me because of you, and my life will be spared on your account."

¹⁴ When Abram entered Egypt, the Egyptians saw that the woman was very beautiful. ¹⁵ Pharaoh's officials saw her and praised her to Pharaoh, so the woman was taken to Pharaoh's household. ¹⁶ He treated Abram well because of her, and Abram acquired flocks and herds, male and female donkeys, male and female slaves, and camels.

¹⁷ But the LORD struck Pharaoh and his household with severe plagues because of Abram's wife, Sarai. ¹⁸ So Pharaoh sent for Abram and said, "What have you done to me? Why didn't you tell me she was your wife? ¹⁹ Why did you say, 'She's my sister,' so that I took her as my wife? Now, here is your wife. Take her and go!" ²⁰ Then Pharaoh gave his men orders about him, and they sent him away with his wife and all he had.

GENESIS 15:1-6

¹ After these events, the word of the LORD came to Abram in a vision:

> Do not be afraid, Abram.
> I am your shield;
> your reward will be very great.

² But Abram said, "LORD God, what can you give me, since I am childless and the heir of my house is Eliezer of Damascus?" ³ Abram continued, "Look, you have given me no offspring, so a slave born in my house will be my heir."

⁴ Now the word of the LORD came to him: "This one will not be your heir; instead, one who comes from your own body will be your heir." ⁵ He took him outside and said, "Look at the sky and count the stars, if you are able to count them." Then he said to him, "Your offspring will be that numerous."

⁶ Abram believed the LORD, and he credited it to him as righteousness.

GENESIS 16:1-6

1 Abram's wife, Sarai, had not borne any children for him, but she owned an Egyptian slave named Hagar. 2 Sarai said to Abram, "Since the LORD has prevented me from bearing children, go to my slave; perhaps through her I can build a family." And Abram agreed to what Sarai said. 3 So Abram's wife, Sarai, took Hagar, her Egyptian slave, and gave her to her husband, Abram, as a wife for him. This happened after Abram had lived in the land of Canaan ten years. 4 He slept with Hagar, and she became pregnant. When she saw that she was pregnant, her mistress became contemptible to her. 5 Then Sarai said to Abram, "You are responsible for my suffering! I put my slave in your arms, and when she saw that she was pregnant, I became contemptible to her. May the LORD judge between me and you."

6 Abram replied to Sarai, "Here, your slave is in your power; do whatever you want with her." Then Sarai mistreated her so much that she ran away from her.

GENESIS 17:1-8, 15-19

1 When Abram was ninety-nine years old, the LORD appeared to him, saying, "I am God Almighty. Live in my presence and be blameless. 2 I will set up my covenant between me and you, and I will multiply you greatly."

3 Then Abram fell facedown and God spoke with him: 4 "As for me, here is my covenant with you: You will become the father of many nations. 5 Your name will no longer be Abram; your name will be Abraham, for I will make you the father of many nations. 6 I will make you extremely fruitful and will make nations and kings come from you.

7 I will confirm my covenant that is between me and you and your future offspring throughout their generations. It is a permanent covenant to be your God and the God of your offspring after you. 8 And to you and your future offspring I will give the land where you are residing — all the land of Canaan — as a permanent possession, and I will be their God."

...

15 God said to Abraham, "As for your wife Sarai, do not call her Sarai, for Sarah will be her name. 16 I will bless her; indeed, I will give you a son by her. I will bless her, and she will produce nations; kings of peoples will come from her."

17 Abraham fell facedown. Then he laughed and said to himself, "Can a child be born to a hundred-year-old man? Can Sarah, a ninety-year-old woman, give birth?"

18 So Abraham said to God, "If only Ishmael were acceptable to you!"

19 But God said, "No. Your wife Sarah will bear you a son, and you will name him Isaac. I will confirm my covenant with him as a permanent covenant for his future offspring.

GENESIS 18:10-15

10 The LORD said, "I will certainly come back to you in about a year's time, and your wife Sarah will have a son!" Now Sarah was listening at the entrance of the tent behind him.

11 Abraham and Sarah were old and getting on in years. Sarah had passed the age of childbearing. 12 So she laughed to herself: "After I am worn out and my lord is old, will I have delight?"

13 But the LORD asked Abraham, "Why did Sarah laugh, saying, 'Can I really have a baby when I'm old? ' 14 Is anything impossible for the LORD? At the appointed time I will come back to you, and in about a year she will have a son."

15 Sarah denied it. "I did not laugh," she said, because she was afraid.

But he replied, "No, you did laugh."

GENESIS 21:1-7

1 The LORD came to Sarah as he had said, and the LORD did for Sarah what he had promised. 2 Sarah became pregnant and bore a son to Abraham in his old age, at the appointed time God had told him. 3 Abraham named his son who was born to him — the one Sarah bore to him — Isaac. 4 When his son Isaac was eight days old, Abraham circumcised him, as God had commanded him. 5 Abraham was a hundred years old when his son Isaac was born to him.

6 Sarah said, "God has made me laugh, and everyone who hears will laugh with me." 7 She also said, "Who would have told Abraham that Sarah would nurse children? Yet I have borne a son for him in his old age."

Lesson 2 Questions

1. God speaks to Abraham on several occasions, each time clarifying the covenant (a formal, legal arrangement) he intends to make with Abraham's family. List out the key details of the promise God makes to Abraham and Sarah. What do these promises teach us about God?

2. Abraham and Sarah make some choices in their marriage that might seem a little strange, to put it mildly! The couple is looking for a solution to an impossible problem, and just like Adam and Eve, they must choose between God's way or what seems right in their own eyes. Make a list of the ways they try to preserve a family legacy by their own efforts. What does God do instead?

3. Abraham subjects Sarah to an Egyptian harem out of fear for his own safety (he repeats this deception in Genesis 20 with another king). How does God intervene? How might this experience add further pain to her barrenness?

4. Circle the references to laughter throughout the story. Don't forget to include Isaac's name, which translates to "he laughs." What is the motivation for laughter when it is first mentioned in the story? How does Sarah's view of laughter evolve with the birth of her son? Does her laughter change anything about the promise God made? Why or why not?

5. The New Testament letter to the Hebrews extols the faith of Sarah. Read about her in Hebrews 11:1–12. What actions does she take that reveal her faith? What personal experiences does she live through that would require faith? How might these have led her to trust that God would be faithful in bringing laughter to her old age?

6. Chart out your faith journey. What key milestones in your life have grown your faith?

7. Sometimes we can get so caught up in the miraculous birth of Isaac to a post-menopausal woman that we forget that having more children than stars in the sky is a promise with a purpose—God blesses Sarah's family *so that they can be a blessing*. Consider the miracles and blessings in your own life. How might God be calling you to use those blessings to bless others?

8. *El-roi*, the God Who Sees, sees not only Hagar, but also Abraham and Sarah in all their imperfections. What is your reaction to knowing that God sees you?

Lesson 2
Prayer

What promises from Scripture do you struggle to believe? What often gets in the way and what solutions have you tried? Take some time to pray that God would show you how he plans to fulfill his promises.

What are God's promises?

Some of them can be found here: Deuteronomy 31:6, Psalm 46:1, Ephesians 1:7–8, Colossians 1:13–14, Isaiah 40:28–29, Matthew 11:28–30, John 16:33, Romans 6:14, Isaiah 26:3

What God promises	The problem

My solution	Prayer for God's solution

Leah

Character Portrait

Who	Jacob's first wife and the mother of six of his sons, including Levi and Judah, and his daughter
When	Middle Bronze Age, 2000–1800 BC
Where	Haran, the territory of Laban's clan

Study Tool
Meditation Literature — *Harnessing Our Imagination*

We've already considered how the Bible is written as meditation literature, a group of thoughtfully arranged stories that we can ponder again and again. One way that we are invited to meditate on God's story is to allow our imaginations to fill in some of the narrative gaps. As you read about Leah and her sister Rachel, consider what you've learned so far about the culture of the Bible and imagine the unwritten scenes in their story. Use discernment in this creative exercise, though. Pay close attention to what *is* included in the story and align your wonderings with specific details in the text. For example, if a person expresses a certain emotion, expect honesty rather than sarcasm, unless there is a clear reason to assume otherwise. If she makes a particular decision, consider what feelings and experiences would be in alignment with those actions. By thoughtfully imagining the world in which biblical women lived, we can connect to them more personally and see God's intervention for the truly miraculous act it is. •

Lesson 3
Passage

In this next part of the story, we meet Jacob, the younger of two sons born to Sarah's promised child, Isaac. The second twin to come out of the womb, Jacob crafted a plan with his mother, Rebekah, to deceive Isaac into giving him the blessing reserved for the oldest son. Once he secured his inheritance (and to avoid the murderous intent of his brother), Jacob traveled to the home country of his mother to find a wife among her brother's clan.

Battling for Babies

While the family feud between Leah and Rachel might seem petty to us, we want to consider the stakes. These young wives are vying not only for security and personal worth, ❹ but for the affection of their shared husband. They are so eager to have children that they are willing to use their servants in an ancient form of surrogacy, showing a similar disregard of Zilpah and Bilhah that their father showed to them.

[1] Jacob resumed his journey and went to the eastern country. [2] He looked and saw a well in a field. Three flocks of sheep were lying there beside it because the sheep were watered from this well. But a large stone covered the opening of the well. [3] The shepherds would roll the stone from the opening of the well and water the sheep when all the flocks were gathered there. Then they would return the stone to its place over the well's opening.

[4] Jacob asked the men at the well, "My brothers! Where are you from?"

"We're from Haran," they answered.

[5] "Do you know Laban, Nahor's grandson?" Jacob asked them.

They answered, "We know him."

[6] "Is he well?" Jacob asked.

"Yes," they said, "and here is his daughter Rachel, coming with his sheep."

[7] Then Jacob said, "Look, it is still broad daylight. It's not time for the animals to be gathered. Water the flock, then go out and let them graze." [8] But they replied, "We can't until all the flocks have been gathered and the stone is rolled from the well's opening. Then we will water the sheep."

[9] While he was still speaking with them, Rachel came with her father's sheep, for she was a shepherdess. [10] As soon as Jacob saw his uncle Laban's daughter Rachel with his sheep, he went up and rolled the stone from the opening and watered his uncle Laban's sheep. [11] Then Jacob kissed Rachel and wept loudly. [12] He told Rachel that he was her father's relative, Rebekah's son. She ran and told her father.

JACOB DECEIVED

[13] When Laban heard the news about his sister's son Jacob, he ran to meet him, hugged him, and kissed him. Then he took him to his house, and Jacob told him all that had happened.

[14] Laban said to him, "Yes, you are my own flesh and blood."

After Jacob had stayed with him a month, [15] Laban said to him, "Just because you're my relative, should you work for me for nothing? Tell me what your wages should be."

[16] Now Laban had two daughters: the older was named Leah, and the younger was named Rachel. [17] Leah had tender eyes, but Rachel was shapely and beautiful. [18] Jacob loved Rachel, so he answered Laban, "I'll work for you seven years for your younger daughter Rachel."

¹⁹ Laban replied, "Better that I give her to you than to some other man. Stay with me."
²⁰ So Jacob worked seven years for Rachel, and they seemed like only a few days to him because of his love for her.

²¹ Then Jacob said to Laban, "Since my time is complete, give me my wife, so I can sleep with her." ²² So Laban invited all the men of the place and sponsored a feast. ²³ That evening, Laban took his daughter Leah and gave her to Jacob, and he slept with her. ²⁴ And Laban gave his slave Zilpah to his daughter Leah as her slave.

²⁵ When morning came, there was Leah! So he said to Laban, "What have you done to me? Wasn't it for Rachel that I worked for you? Why have you deceived me?"

²⁶ Laban answered, "It is not the custom in our country to give the younger daughter in marriage before the firstborn. ²⁷ Complete this week of wedding celebration, and we will also give you this younger one in return for working yet another seven years for me."

²⁸ And Jacob did just that. He finished the week of celebration, and Laban gave him his daughter Rachel as his wife. ²⁹ And Laban gave his slave Bilhah to his daughter Rachel as her slave. ³⁰ Jacob slept with Rachel also, and indeed, he loved Rachel more than Leah. And he worked for Laban another seven years.

JACOB'S SONS

³¹ When the LORD saw that Leah was neglected, he opened her womb; but Rachel was unable to conceive. ³² Leah conceived, gave birth to a son, and named him Reuben, for she said, "The LORD has seen my affliction; surely my husband will love me now."

³³ She conceived again, gave birth to a son, and said, "The LORD heard that I am neglected and has given me this son also." So she named him Simeon.

³⁴ She conceived again, gave birth to a son, and said, "At last, my husband will become attached to me because I have borne three sons for him." Therefore he was named Levi.

³⁵ And she conceived again, gave birth to a son, and said, "This time I will praise the LORD." Therefore she named him Judah. Then Leah stopped having children.

GENESIS 30:1-24

¹ When Rachel saw that she was not bearing Jacob any children, she envied her sister. "Give me sons, or I will die!" she said to Jacob.

² Jacob became angry with Rachel and said, "Am I in the place of God? He has withheld offspring from you!"

³ Then she said, "Here is my maid Bilhah. Go sleep with her, and she'll bear children for me so that through her I too can build a family." ⁴ So Rachel gave her slave Bilhah to Jacob as a wife, and he slept with her. ⁵ Bilhah conceived and bore Jacob a son.

Sharing the Mandrakes

After all the back and forth in this battle of the babies, the story of Reuben's mandrakes interrupts the cycle. On one hand, Rachel has become so desperate for her own children that she is willing to barter intimacy with Jacob for a flower believed to promote fertility.[9] These mandrakes, however, represent so much more. Young Reuben found the flowers and offered them to his mother, Leah, as a gift. Leah finds Rachel's request insulting because her sister is asking to share in the delight of motherhood when Rachel already has the sole favor of their husband. Leah may not be able to enjoy her marriage, but she does have the pleasure of her children's love. Here, Rachel makes a surprising choice. Rather than hoard Jacob's attention, she offers a truce. She will share the marriage bed if Leah will consider sharing the joys of mothering.[10]

6 Rachel said, "God has vindicated me; yes, he has heard me and given me a son," so she named him Dan.

7 Rachel's slave Bilhah conceived again and bore Jacob a second son. 8 Rachel said, "In my wrestlings with God, I have wrestled with my sister and won," and she named him Naphtali.

9 When Leah saw that she had stopped having children, she took her slave Zilpah and gave her to Jacob as a wife. 10 Leah's slave Zilpah bore Jacob a son. 11 Then Leah said, "What good fortune!" and she named him Gad.

12 When Leah's slave Zilpah bore Jacob a second son, 13 Leah said, "I am happy that the women call me happy," so she named him Asher.

14 Reuben went out during the wheat harvest and found some mandrakes in the field. When he brought them to his mother Leah, Rachel asked, "Please give me some of your son's mandrakes."

15 But Leah replied to her, "Isn't it enough that you have taken my husband? Now you also want to take my son's mandrakes?"

"Well then," Rachel said, "he can sleep with you tonight in exchange for your son's mandrakes."

16 When Jacob came in from the field that evening, Leah went out to meet him and said, "You must come with me, for I have hired you with my son's mandrakes." So Jacob slept with her that night.

17 God listened to Leah, and she conceived and bore Jacob a fifth son. 18 Leah said, "God has rewarded me for giving my slave to my husband," and she named him Issachar.

19 Then Leah conceived again and bore Jacob a sixth son. 20 "God has given me a good gift," Leah said. "This time my husband will honor me because I have borne six sons for him," and she named him Zebulun. 21 Later, Leah bore a daughter and named her Dinah.

22 Then God remembered Rachel. He listened to her and opened her womb. 23 She conceived and bore a son, and she said, "God has taken away my disgrace." 24 She named him Joseph and said, "May the LORD add another son to me."

The LORD *has* **seen** *my affliction...*

Genesis 39:32

Family Tree

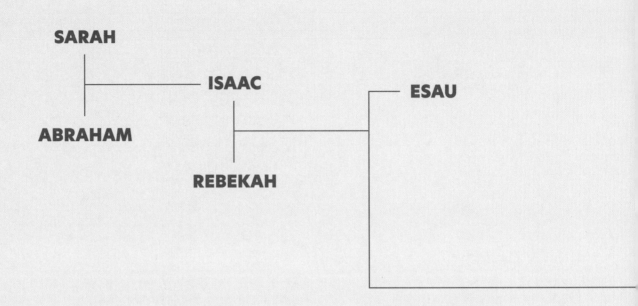

SARAH

ISAAC

ESAU

ABRAHAM

REBEKAH

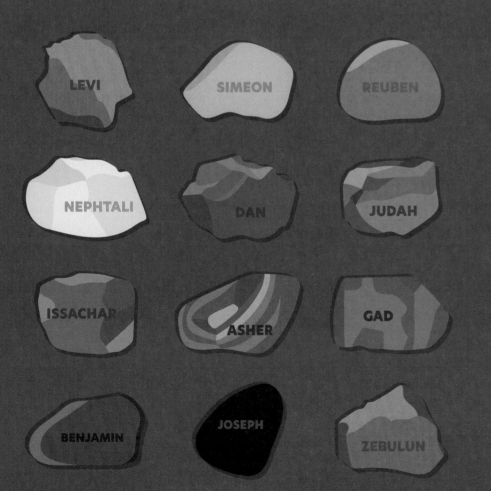

LEVI

SIMEON

REUBEN

NEPHTALI

DAN

JUDAH

ISSACHAR

ASHER

GAD

BENJAMIN

JOSEPH

ZEBULUN

All future High Priests in Israel wore a breastplate inlaid with twelve gemstones, one for each son of Judah.

[17] Place a setting of gemstones on it, four rows of stones:

The first row should be a row of carnelian, topaz, and emerald; [18] the second row, a turquoise, a lapis lazuli, and a diamond; [19] the third row, a jacinth, an agate, and an amethyst; [20] and the fourth row, a beryl, an onyx, and a jasper.

They should be adorned with gold filigree in their settings. [21] The twelve stones are to correspond to the names of Israel's sons. Each stone must be engraved like a seal, with one of the names of the twelve tribes.

Exodus 28:17–21

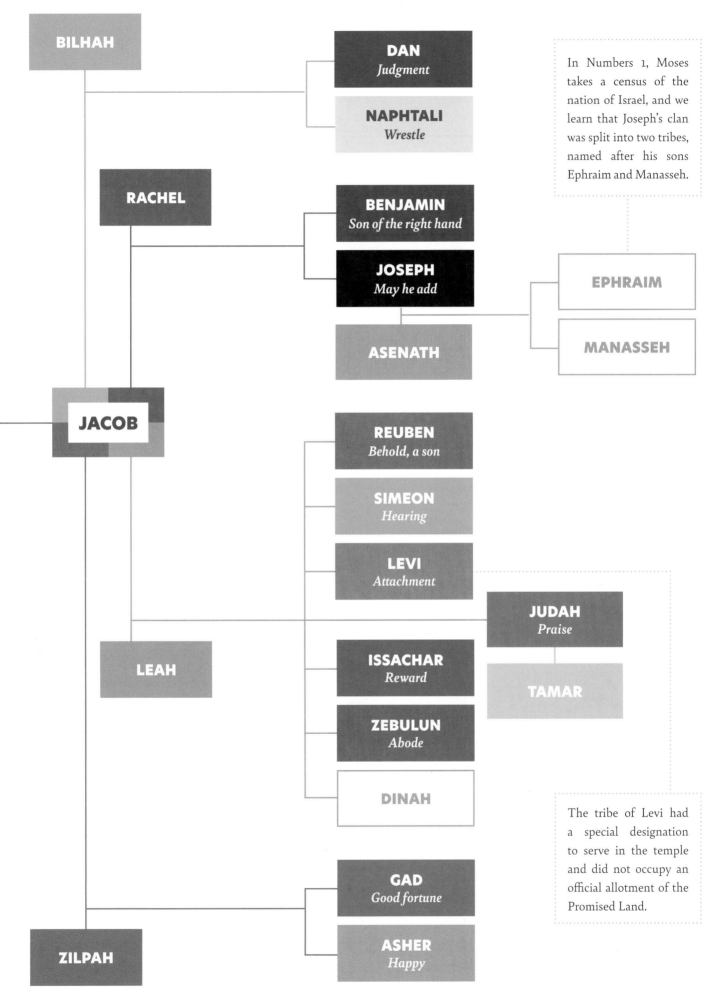

BILHAH

DAN
Judgment

NAPHTALI
Wrestle

In Numbers 1, Moses takes a census of the nation of Israel, and we learn that Joseph's clan was split into two tribes, named after his sons Ephraim and Manasseh.

RACHEL

BENJAMIN
Son of the right hand

JOSEPH
May he add

EPHRAIM

MANASSEH

ASENATH

JACOB

REUBEN
Behold, a son

SIMEON
Hearing

LEVI
Attachment

JUDAH
Praise

ISSACHAR
Reward

TAMAR

ZEBULUN
Abode

DINAH

The tribe of Levi had a special designation to serve in the temple and did not occupy an official allotment of the Promised Land.

LEAH

GAD
Good fortune

ASHER
Happy

ZILPAH

Lesson 3 Questions

1. Laban is responsible for finding husbands for his two daughters.  When he considers Jacob's offer, he expresses his preference for Rachel to wed a member of his own clan, rather than a foreign husband. Then, he makes a switch. In what ways does his act of deception provide for his older daughter, Leah? In what ways does it harm or disregard her?

2. A popular rabbinic interpretation suggests that Leah's "tender eyes" are evidence of a life of mourning. Because her aunt Rebekah had two sons, the likeliest marriage prospect for her as the oldest daughter would be the older son Esau, who had a reputation for being careless and wicked.[11] Knowing this, in what ways might Leah's life embody the meaning of her name, "weary"? How does God respond to her prayers?

3. **Jacob makes it clear from the beginning that he loves Rachel. During the seven years he works in the family business, Leah would have seen the way he interacted with Rachel. What are some ways this experience could have affected Leah? What are some possible reasons for her silence? Who are the decision makers for Leah at different points in the story?**

4. Take some time to imagine the details surrounding Jacob's wedding. Jacob is tricked into marrying the wrong woman; once he discovers the deception, he still has to go back to the party for another week. At the end of that week, Laban lets him take Rachel as a second wife, but we do not hear anything about a wedding for her. What do you think those first weeks of marriage felt like for Leah? For Rachel?

5. Both women in this story believe that Jacob is their rightful husband. What case can each woman make?

Leah	Rachel

6. Take a look at the family tree on page 36-37 and read through the translations for each son's name. What do we learn about Leah by the names she gives her sons and those born through Zilpah? ❹ How do the names show Leah's view of herself and of God?

7. Are you in the middle of a rivalry like Leah and Rachel—each stuck in your own camp? In what ways might God be calling you to reconcile? How can you pursue peace even if you still disagree?

8. Leah and Rachel's story echoes Sarah and Hagar's in their attempt to control fertility, this time to a preposterous degree. Who is truly in charge of their fertility? In what area of your life do you struggle most with wanting to control the outcome? How does this impact the way you treat others and how you think about God?

9. In Leviticus 18, God gives a set of laws to Moses (we will meet him in Part Two) about appropriate sexual relationships. The rules require the Israelites to live in a way that sets them apart from the Canaanites and Egyptians. Verse 18 specifically forbids a man "to marry a woman as a rival to her sister." Given the story of Rachel and Leah, how could certain restrictions like this actually provide freedom? What other rules in the Bible do you think of as restrictive or unfair? What details in this story might cause you to rethink your opinion?

Lesson 3
Prayer

God listens to the weary one. If this is you today, take some time to share with God all the burdens that are making you weary. Praise God for ways he has redeemed the weariness in your past.

Rachel

Character Portrait

Who	The second and favored wife of Jacob, mother to Joseph (Jacob's favorite son) and Benjamin
When	Middle Bronze Age, 2000–1800 BC
Where	Haran, the territory of Laban's clan

Study Tool
Character Speech — *What do the women say?*

Silence surrounding the lives and experiences of women is a frustrating reality for historians. The records of ancient cultures are limited by what the people of the time felt was valuable to preserve. Even as recent as the early 1900s, archeologists who explored famous historical sites had a habit of throwing away materials like woven cloth that might have given us clues to the lives of women.[12] Being able to actually read their recorded speech is a powerful tool to help us lay aside our Western, 21st-century perspectives and better understand their lives.

The Bible includes much more information about women than literature of the same time period, and where other books reference women, we learn only the male author's opinion of them. By contrast, the words of Scripture do not only speak *about* women. They allow women to speak for themselves. Some people may find the words of women insignificant, but God does not. He has much to teach us about his design for women if we are willing to hear what the women in the Bible have to say. •

Lesson 4
Passage

We met Rachel in the last lesson. Now that Jacob's family has grown in size, he longs to return to the land of his mother and father. His relationship with Laban continues to sour as they squabble over which part of the flock Jacob may be permitted to take for his wages.

Seeking Justice

Scholars have suggested a few reasons for Rachel's theft. Perhaps she found some personal significance in these household idols or recognized their financial value.[13] Or maybe she hoped that these gods would grant her fertility. **7** In any case, she viewed them as a rightful part of her inheritance.

In the original Hebrew, Rachel's statement about menstruation operates as careful doublespeak. A closer English translation reads, "I cannot rise before you, for I have the way of women." In one sense, Rachel is claiming that ritual cleansing laws prevent her from standing up, lest her father become unclean by touching her during the time of her period. However, the term "rise before you" is used elsewhere in Scripture to describe legal confrontation. So she is also saying that as a woman, she is unable to bring a legal charge against her father for withholding her inheritance.[14]

Rachel's speech and actions are an act of rebellion against the injustice she believes was done to her. While men during this time often made decisions that neglected women's well-being, God does not.[15] Setting right the injustices of our sinful world is part of the great redemption he has planned in Christ.

³ The LORD said to him, "Go back to the land of your ancestors and to your family, and I will be with you."

⁴ Jacob had Rachel and Leah called to the field where his flocks were. ⁵ He said to them, "I can see from your father's face that his attitude toward me is not the same as before, but the God of my father has been with me. ⁶ You know that with all my strength I have served your father ⁷ and that he has cheated me and changed my wages ten times. But God has not let him harm me. ⁸ If he said, 'The spotted sheep will be your wages,' then all the sheep were born spotted. If he said, 'The streaked sheep will be your wages,' then all the sheep were born streaked. ⁹ God has taken away your father's herds and given them to me.

¹⁰ "When the flocks were breeding, I saw in a dream that the streaked, spotted, and speckled males were mating with the females. ¹¹ In that dream the angel of God said to me, 'Jacob! ' and I said, 'Here I am.' ¹² And he said, 'Look up and see: all the males that are mating with the flocks are streaked, spotted, and speckled, for I have seen all that Laban has been doing to you. ¹³ I am the God of Bethel, where you poured oil on the stone marker and made a solemn vow to me. Get up, leave this land, and return to your native land.'"

¹⁴ Then Rachel and Leah answered him, "Do we have any portion or inheritance in our father's family? ¹⁵ Are we not regarded by him as outsiders? For he has sold us and has certainly spent our purchase price. ¹⁶ In fact, all the wealth that God has taken away from our father belongs to us and to our children. So do whatever God has said to you."

¹⁷ So Jacob got up and put his children and wives on the camels. ¹⁸ He took all the livestock and possessions he had acquired in Paddan-aram, and he drove his herds to go to the land of Canaan, to his father Isaac. ¹⁹ When Laban had gone to shear his sheep, Rachel stole her father's household idols. ²⁰ And Jacob deceived Laban the Aramean, not telling him that he was fleeing. ²¹ He fled with all his possessions, crossed the Euphrates, and headed for the hill country of Gilead.

LABAN OVERTAKES JACOB

²² On the third day Laban was told that Jacob had fled. ²³ So he took his relatives with him, pursued Jacob for seven days, and overtook him in the hill country of Gilead. ²⁴ But God came to Laban the Aramean in a dream at night. "Watch yourself!" God warned him. "Don't say anything to Jacob, either good or bad."

²⁵ When Laban overtook Jacob, Jacob had pitched his tent in the hill country, and Laban and his relatives also pitched their tents in the hill country of Gilead. ²⁶ Laban said to Jacob, "What have you done? You have deceived me and taken my daughters away like prisoners of war! ²⁷ Why did you secretly flee from me, deceive me, and not tell me? I would have sent you away with joy and singing, with tambourines and lyres, ²⁸ but you didn't even let me kiss my grandchildren and my daughters. You have acted foolishly. ²⁹ I could do you

great harm, but last night the God of your father said to me, 'Watch yourself! Don't say anything to Jacob, either good or bad.' 30 Now you have gone off because you long for your father's family — but why have you stolen my gods?"

31 Jacob answered, "I was afraid, for I thought you would take your daughters from me by force. 32 If you find your gods with anyone here, he will not live! Before our relatives, point out anything that is yours and take it." Jacob did not know that Rachel had stolen the idols.

33 So Laban went into Jacob's tent, Leah's tent, and the tents of the two concubines, but he found nothing. When he left Leah's tent, he went into Rachel's tent. 34 Now Rachel had taken Laban's household idols, put them in the saddlebag of the camel, and sat on them. Laban searched the whole tent but found nothing.

35 She said to her father, "Don't be angry, my lord, that I cannot stand up in your presence; I am having my period." So Laban searched, but could not find the household idols.

JACOB'S COVENANT WITH LABAN

36 Then Jacob became incensed and brought charges against Laban. "What is my crime?" he said to Laban. "What is my sin, that you have pursued me? 37 You've searched all my possessions! Have you found anything of yours? Put it here before my relatives and yours, and let them decide between the two of us. 38 I've been with you these twenty years. Your ewes and female goats have not miscarried, and I have not eaten the rams from your flock. 39 I did not bring you any of the flock torn by wild beasts; I myself bore the loss. You demanded payment from me for what was stolen by day or by night. 40 There I was — the heat consumed me by day and the frost by night, and sleep fled from my eyes. 41 For twenty years in your household I served you — fourteen years for your two daughters and six years for your flocks — and you have changed my wages ten times! 42 If the God of my father, the God of Abraham, the Fear of Isaac, had not been with me, certainly now you would have sent me off empty-handed. But God has seen my affliction and my hard work, and he issued his verdict last night."

43 Then Laban answered Jacob, "The daughters are my daughters; the children, my children; and the flocks, my flocks! Everything you see is mine! But what can I do today for these daughters of mine or for the children they have borne? 44 Come now, let's make a covenant, you and I. Let it be a witness between the two of us."

45 So Jacob picked out a stone and set it up as a marker. 46 Then Jacob said to his relatives, "Gather stones." And they took stones and made a mound, then ate there by the mound. 47 Laban named the mound Jegar-sahadutha, but Jacob named it Galeed.

48 Then Laban said, "This mound is a witness between you and me today." Therefore the place was called Galeed 49 and also Mizpah, for he said, "May the LORD watch between you and me when we are out of each other's sight. 50 If you mistreat my daughters or take other wives, though no one is with us, understand that God will be a witness between you and me." 51 Laban also said to Jacob, "Look at this mound and the marker I have set up between you and me. 52 This mound is a witness and the marker is a witness that I will not pass beyond this mound to you, and you will not pass beyond this mound and this marker to do me harm. 53 The God of Abraham, and the gods of Nahor — the gods of their father — will judge between us." And Jacob swore by the Fear of his father Isaac. 54 Then Jacob offered a sacrifice on the mountain and invited his relatives to eat a meal. So they ate a meal and spent the night on the mountain. 55 Laban got up early in the morning, kissed his grandchildren and daughters, and blessed them. Then Laban left to return home.

GENESIS 35:16-20

16 They set out from Bethel. When they were still some distance from Ephrath, Rachel began to give birth, and her labor was difficult. 17 During her difficult labor, the midwife said to her, "Don't be afraid, for you have another son." 18 With her last breath — for she was dying — she named him Ben-oni, but his father called him Benjamin. 19 So Rachel died and was buried on the way to Ephrath (that is, Bethlehem). 20 Jacob set up a marker on her grave; it is the marker at Rachel's grave still today.

Lesson 4 Questions

1. Yesterday's passage revealed that Rachel is a shepherdess. ❺ What do you think this job entails? How does this impact your imagination about her day-to-day life?

2. **Rachel is the favorite wife, but her situation is far from perfect. List specific details from yesterday and today's readings that reveal her personal struggles. How do these trials contribute to her feelings toward her father?**

3. What changes in Rachel's life after she heals the rift with her sister? What now unites the sisters?

4. When Laban catches up to Jacob's fleeing family, what does he give as the reason for his anger? Do his actions support or contradict his words?

5. **Rachel and Leah are caught in a whirlwind of deception. Prior to meeting his wives, Jacob uses deception to steal the birthright from his older brother and a blessing from his father. Then, Jacob is deceived by his father-in-law on multiple occasions. What might we admire or advise against in Rachel's strategically worded conversation with Laban? What is the difference—if any—between wise cunning and evil deception?**

6. Rachel is stuck in a social structure that doesn't allow her the freedom to publicly challenge her father or advocate for her inheritance. What options does she have, and what does she ultimately decide to do? What would you have chosen?

7. In this story, we have considered what a person's words tell us about them. Think about the words you've used in the last week. What did they reveal about your character?

8. **God promises that one day he will restore the earth to its Edenic state where we can all live under his perfect justice. In the meantime, like Rachel, we long for justice in a world that is routinely unfair. How does your own story point you to a need for God's justice?**

9. Rachel dies before seeing her sons grow up, but both become honorable men. ❻ Like her, Joseph would experience great cruelty—being sold into slavery by his brothers, seduced by his boss's wife, and enslaved in Egypt—and yet he saves Jacob's entire family from a famine. You can read Joseph's story in Genesis 37 and 39-47. Both Rachel and her sons had imperfect lives in the context of an imperfect family. How do their stories impact your view of your own family? What does God do in the midst of imperfection for those who are faithful to him?

Lesson 4
Prayer

God hears even our wildest requests. List specific prayers for justice in your spheres of influence.

My home	My workplace or school

My city	The world

Tamar

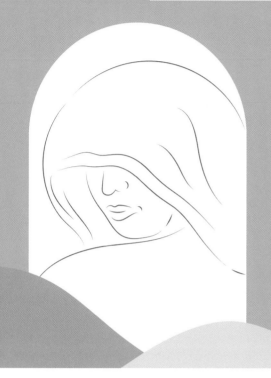

Character Portrait

Who	The daughter-in-law of Judah and mother of twins, Perez and Zerah
When	1800–1650 BC
Where	Canaan

Study Tool

Story Arrangement — *What does the author say?*

The Bible is composed of sixty-six books that contain multiple literary genres—songs and poetry, instruction, allegory, history, and narrative. All of Scripture is the Word of God that he inspired human writers to compose and arrange for the rest of us. As we look specifically at the narratives of women in the Bible, we should pay attention to all the details the biblical author includes. In any record of history, the writer determines what parts of the story are significant enough to make it into the final draft, so it is no accident when an author repeats certain phrases or adds vivid detail.

As much as these stories are the history of God's people, they are also beautifully arranged literature. Or viewed another way, the Bible is like a symphony. Think about the soundtrack to your favorite movie. Have you ever noticed that there are certain musical riffs that repeat every time a particular character comes on screen? In music, these are called *leitmotifs*, and they mirror what happens in literature. As you are listening to Scripture, pay attention to how the story picks up phrases or themes throughout. •

Lesson 5 Passage

This part of the story focuses on one of Jacob's twelve sons, Judah, the fourth son of Leah. His family, the tribe of Judah, will include King David and ultimately Jesus. But in order for that to happen, Tamar will face some complicated obstacles.

¹ At that time Judah left his brothers and settled near an Adullamite named Hirah. ² There Judah saw the daughter of a Canaanite named Shua; he took her as a wife and slept with her. ³ She conceived and gave birth to a son, and he named him Er. ⁴ She conceived again, gave birth to a son, and named him Onan. ⁵ She gave birth to another son and named him Shelah. It was at Chezib that she gave birth to him.

⁶ Judah got a wife for Er, his firstborn, and her name was Tamar. ⁷ Now Er, Judah's firstborn, was evil in the Lord's sight, and the Lord put him to death. ⁸ Then Judah said to Onan, "Sleep with your brother's wife. Perform your duty as her brother-in-law and produce offspring for your brother." ⁹ But Onan knew that the offspring would not be his, so whenever he slept with his brother's wife, he released his semen on the ground so that he would not produce offspring for his brother. ¹⁰ What he did was evil in the Lord's sight, so he put him to death also.

¹¹ Then Judah said to his daughter-in-law Tamar, "Remain a widow in your father's house until my son Shelah grows up." For he thought, "He might die too, like his brothers." So Tamar went to live in her father's house.

¹² After a long time Judah's wife, the daughter of Shua, died. When Judah had finished mourning, he and his friend Hirah the Adullamite went up to Timnah to his sheepshearers. ¹³ Tamar was told, "Your father-in-law is going up to Timnah to shear his sheep." ¹⁴ So she took off her widow's clothes, veiled her face, covered herself, and sat at the entrance to Enaim, which is on the way to Timnah. For she saw that, though Shelah had grown up, she had not been given to him as a wife. ¹⁵ When Judah saw her, he thought she was a prostitute, for she had covered her face.

¹⁶ He went over to her and said, "Come, let me sleep with you," for he did not know that she was his daughter-in-law.

She said, "What will you give me for sleeping with me?"

¹⁷ "I will send you a young goat from my flock," he replied.

But she said, "Only if you leave something with me until you send it."

¹⁸ "What should I give you?" he asked. She answered, "Your signet ring, your cord, and the staff in your hand." So he gave them to her and slept with her, and she became pregnant by him. ¹⁹ She got up and left, then removed her veil and put her widow's clothes back on.

²⁰ When Judah sent the young goat by his friend the Adullamite in order to get back the items he had left with the woman, he could not find her. ²¹ He asked the men of the place, "Where is the cult prostitute who was beside the road at Enaim?"

"There has been no cult prostitute here," they answered.

22 So the Adullamite returned to Judah, saying, "I couldn't find her, and besides, the men of the place said, 'There has been no cult prostitute here.'"

23 Judah replied, "Let her keep the items for herself; otherwise we will become a laughingstock. After all, I did send this young goat, but you couldn't find her."

24 About three months later Judah was told, "Your daughter-in-law, Tamar, has been acting like a prostitute, and now she is pregnant."

"Bring her out," Judah said, "and let her be burned to death!"

25 As she was being brought out, she sent her father-in-law this message: "I am pregnant by the man to whom these items belong." And she added, "Examine them. Whose signet ring, cord, and staff are these?"

26 Judah recognized them and said, "She is more in the right than I, since I did not give her to my son Shelah." And he did not know her intimately again.

27 When the time came for her to give birth, there were twins in her womb. 28 As she was giving birth, one of them put out his hand, and the midwife took it and tied a scarlet thread around it, announcing, "This one came out first." 29 But then he pulled his hand back, out came his brother, and she said, "What a breakout you have made for yourself!" So he was named Perez. 30 Then his brother, who had the scarlet thread tied to his hand, came out, and was named Zerah.

What is the brother-in-law's duty?

The duty of the brother-in-law mentioned in this passage would later be codified in the Mosaic Law as "Levirate marriage."[16] A brother was obligated to care for his sibling's widow by producing an heir with her who could inherit the deceased brother's land. Doing so not only secured the family's legacy, but was also a protective grace to the widow who would now have a child to care for her in old age. ❹

In similar customs of the period, the deceased man's father could perform the Levirate duty if he did not have another son who was old enough. Or he could declare the woman a widow, so that she might be free to marry another man. By promising to someday give her his youngest son, Judah leaves Tamar in limbo.[17] She continues to age as she waits for a third husband to grow into adulthood.

Lesson 5 Questions

1. **Consider Judah's speech and actions toward Tamar in three different moments of the story. How does the author want us to view Judah's choices?**

When Judah meets Tamar disguised as a prostitute	When Judah learns Tamar is pregnant	When Judah learns that he's the father

2. What details in the story does the reader know that are hidden from Judah? How do those details influence the mood of the story and how we view its ultimate outcome?

3. The duty of the brother-in-law was meant to preserve the family line. What were the potential risks of Tamar's plan? What other, safer choices could she have made if she were not committed to this goal?

4. **Judah takes Tamar to trial for prostitution, knowing full well that he has also slept with someone who was not his wife. When Tamar confronts his double standard, what does Judah say? What does his reaction reveal about the way we should understand Tamar's action?**

5. Are you starting to hear Eve's theme in these stories? At least for this moment, Tamar has outwitted the snake[18] and earns an honorable place in Jesus' lineage. Who are the snakes in your life? What might outwitting their deception look like?

6. The author is clear that God condemns Onan for using Tamar for his own pleasure and deliberately withholding her opportunity to conceive. In a parallel way, Hagar, Zilpah, and Bilhah were used by their masters only for their birthing capacity. How do the stories of these women and their influence in the family of Israel help us better understand how God sees them? What hope do they offer for women who have been used for another's pleasure?

7. Tamar wisely secures proof of paternity and waits until her public trial to confront Judah.[19] How does her story inform your idea of wisdom?

8. Judah allowed another household to take care of the woman who should have been his to protect,[20] ❶ while Tamar took action to protect herself and her family's lineage. Think about the people God has called you to protect. What risks or challenges might God want you to take for their sake?

Lesson 5
Prayer

The Bible confronts and condemns all forms of mistreatment and abuse. Pray for the Lord to bring any of this harm to light in your own community. Pray for healing for anyone you know who might be suffering in ways small or large.

Thematic Recap

In Part One we looked at the matriarchs who birthed the nation of Israel. Before we follow them into Egypt, let's take a pause and consider the road we have traveled thus far. What themes have resonated with you most deeply? What have you learned or re-examined? Below is a list of just a few of the topics we've covered. Take some time to reflect on these or any other topics that have been meaningful in your study.

About God	*About Womanhood*	*About Myself*
Shares himself through story	Inclusive mothering	
Values women	Outwitting deception and pursuing wisdom	
Faithful to his promises	Partnering with men for flourishing	
Sees us as we are	Agents of peace	
Loves us despite our sin	God's representatives on earth	

Interlude: *Seeing through the Eyes of a Mother*

I should have died in childbirth at least twice by now. My firstborn put me on bedrest during the final month of pregnancy and my third came during a pandemic. I have thrown up in the bushes outside my office, force fed myself double-butter everything to combat a small-measuring baby, and fallen asleep next to a playing toddler. While some women experience a prenatal glow (and I am truly happy for them!), this was not my lot. But for all the grief, struggle, and stretchmarks, these are my tiny humans, and I wouldn't trade them for all the radiant baby bump pics on the Internet.

As my children began to grow, they added depth to my understanding of women in the Bible. These matriarchs also survived the complications of birth (at least until some didn't) and knew what it felt like to hold minutes-fresh flesh—a tiny, breathing miracle—skin to skin. It was Leah and Tamar who nurtured the fathers of the nation of Israel. Eve and Sarah and Rachel trained up the famous sons in Scripture. I started to mentally footnote who belonged to whom. That's Rachel's firstborn Joseph or Rahab's grandson, Boaz. The emerging truth was so obvious, although I'd been oblivious to it for so long: The famous men in the Bible were raised in the context of a family. They were all mothered.

While the world argues over what it means to be feminine, the Bible offers an embodied word picture. The mother of all living gives birth to all types of living, breathing new mothers. Women in antiquity might have focused on the literal call to be fruitful and multiply, but God's plan has always been about blessing the nations through our spiritual family, whether we have babies of our own or not. That plan is echoed in Jesus' great commission to go and make disciples. The call of mothering is expansive.

Christian women proclaim our God by joining this beautiful lineage of spiritual mothers. Made in his image, we are designed to reflect a God who nurtures us, "as a hen gathers her chicks under her wings."[21] We draw people close to ourselves in a number of ways—physically, emotionally, intellectually, and spiritually—creating the context for life to flourish. We cultivate, nourish, and invest in others, pointing them to the source of wisdom. Spiritual mothers are women who design spaces to promote meaningful relationships within them. Or foster moms and court appointed advocates who welcome society's forgotten children into their homes. Seasoned professionals who sacrifice time to mentor young employees and those same young women who use their social influence to care for God's beautiful creation—they are also spiritual mothers. Mothering looks like a lighting designer clad in a tee and cargo pants who climbs down from the grid to advocate for fair treatment of her crew, or a librarian who makes sure that every child who comes through her doors can find uplifting stories about people who look just like them. Mothering doesn't begin the moment a baby crowns; it's a vocation we can all embody—from child to centenarian—no matter our biological family structure.

And on those days when we feel overwhelmed by this task of spiritual mothering, we are comforted by a God who declares, "Can a woman forget her nursing child, that she should have no compassion on the son of her womb? Even these may forget, yet I will not forget you."[22] We can mother because he first mothered us.

This view of mothering guides the way we look at the women of Scripture. As the children of Tamar, Rachel, Leah, Sarah, and Eve grow into the nation of Israel, they are mentored by the legacy of the great matriarchs and spurred on to faith just as we are by the courageous women in our midst. •

PART TWO

The Wanderers

*His plan was for Adam and Eve to rule together, each using their **unique gifts** to order and nurture God's beautiful world.*

Miram, Shiphrah & Puah

Character Portrait

Miriam	A prophetess and Moses' older sister
Shiphrah & Puah	The midwives who defied Pharaoh
When	Late Bronze age, 1500–1200 BC
Where	Egypt

Study Tool

Patterns — *Strategic Partnerships*

When God created Eve, he designed a necessary ally[23] for Adam. His plan was for Adam and Eve to rule together, each using their unique gifts to order and nurture God's beautiful world. While Adam and Eve's partnership came in the context of marriage, the Bible presents a vision for men and women working together within the family of God at large. Even when the action of a given story seems to focus on a particular man, consider what strategic partnerships with women were essential for the plan to succeed. •

Lesson 6
Passage

The battle of the babies between Leah and Rachel leaves Jacob with a remarkably large family that includes twelve sons. Eleven of these turn on their brother Joseph, who is sold into slavery in Egypt only to rise miraculously into a position of great power that ultimately saves the family during a famine. The family relocates to Egypt where they grow in number. Joseph dies and another pharoah rises to power, who views Joseph's clan as a problem.

The Peril of Dismissing Feminine Strength

The narrative of Moses and the exodus from Egypt is one of the most famous Bible stories. Yet the numerous films and children's Bible depictions don't start where the actual story begins: with the brave resistance of women.

Asking the midwives to kill all the sons of Israel was a serious miscalculation by Pharaoh, who thinks that only the males are a threat to his kingdom. Even as the Hebrew people face fierce oppression, which historically should lead to low birth rates, the strong Hebrew women continue to bear children. Pharaoh fears a rebellion of men and fails to consider the strength that the women display in continuing to birth under such harsh conditions.[24]

EXODUS 1:6-22

⁶ Joseph and all his brothers and all that generation eventually died. ⁷ But the Israelites were fruitful, increased rapidly, multiplied, and became extremely numerous so that the land was filled with them.

⁸ A new king, who did not know about Joseph, came to power in Egypt. ⁹ He said to his people, "Look, the Israelite people are more numerous and powerful than we are. ¹⁰ Come, let's deal shrewdly with them; otherwise they will multiply further, and when war breaks out, they will join our enemies, fight against us, and leave the country." ¹¹ So the Egyptians assigned taskmasters over the Israelites to oppress them with forced labor. They built Pithom and Rameses as supply cities for Pharaoh. ¹² But the more they oppressed them, the more they multiplied and spread so that the Egyptians came to dread the Israelites. ¹³ They worked the Israelites ruthlessly ¹⁴ and made their lives bitter with difficult labor in brick and mortar and in all kinds of fieldwork. They ruthlessly imposed all this work on them.

¹⁵ The king of Egypt said to the Hebrew midwives—the first, whose name was Shiphrah, and the second, whose name was Puah—¹⁶"When you help the Hebrew women give birth, observe them as they deliver. If the child is a son, kill him, but if it's a daughter, she may live." ¹⁷ The midwives, however, feared God and did not do as the king of Egypt had told them; they let the boys live. ¹⁸ So the king of Egypt summoned the midwives and asked them, "Why have you done this and let the boys live?"

¹⁹ The midwives said to Pharaoh, "The Hebrew women are not like the Egyptian women, for they are vigorous and give birth before the midwife can get to them."

²⁰ So God was good to the midwives, and the people multiplied and became very numerous. ²¹ Since the midwives feared God, he gave them families. ²² Pharaoh then commanded all his people, "You must throw every son born to the Hebrews into the Nile, but let every daughter live."

EXODUS 2:1-10

[1] Now a man from the family of Levi married a Levite woman. [2] The woman became pregnant and gave birth to a son; when she saw that he was beautiful, she hid him for three months. [3] But when she could no longer hide him, she got a papyrus basket for him and coated it with asphalt and pitch. She placed the child in it and set it among the reeds by the bank of the Nile. [4] Then his sister stood at a distance in order to see what would happen to him.

[5] Pharaoh's daughter went down to bathe at the Nile while her servant girls walked along the riverbank. She saw the basket among the reeds, sent her slave girl, took it, [6] opened it, and saw him, the child — and there he was, a little boy, crying. She felt sorry for him and said, "This is one of the Hebrew boys." [7] Then his sister said to Pharaoh's daughter, "Should I go and call a Hebrew woman who is nursing to nurse the boy for you?"

[8] "Go," Pharaoh's daughter told her. So the girl went and called the boy's mother. [9] Then Pharaoh's daughter said to her, "Take this child and nurse him for me, and I will pay your wages." So the woman took the boy and nursed him. [10] When the child grew older, she brought him to Pharaoh's daughter, and he became her son. She named him Moses, "Because," she said, "I drew him out of the water."

The Rest of the Story

From here, the story of God's work through Moses—God's appearance in a burning bush, the ten plagues, and the parting of the Red Sea—takes many remarkable turns. Find the full story in Exodus 3–15. God's dramatic rescue of his people is remembered every year in the celebration of Passover.

EXODUS 15:19-21

[19] When Pharaoh's horses with his chariots and horsemen went into the sea, the LORD brought the water of the sea back over them. But the Israelites walked through the sea on dry ground. [20] Then the prophetess Miriam, Aaron's sister, took a tambourine in her hand, and all the women came out following her with tambourines and dancing. [21] Miriam sang to them:

> Sing to the LORD,
> for he is highly exalted;
> he has thrown the horse
> and its rider into the sea.

Lesson 6 Questions

1. The book of Exodus follows the stories we read in Genesis, but opens in Egypt as the beginning of a new narrative arc. What details set the stage for this next part of the story?

Person	Goal	Problem/Obstacle
Pharaoh		
Midwives		
Moses' Mother		

2. Pharaoh seems to think that killing baby boys will solve his population control problem, but it's actually the women who are "exploding" with children[25] and finding ways to subvert his orders. His critical mistake is valuing stereotypically masculine forms of power—physical strength and political prowess. What does this story show us about the kind of people God works through? How might you elevate the contributions of women or others who are currently under the radar?

3. Moses is born into the family of Levi, the priestly tribe. Though flawed in many ways, Moses would speak directly to God, deliver God's law and the rules for the priesthood, and guide the people of Israel to the Promised Land. His brother Aaron would become the first high priest of Israel. How does the involvement of women in Moses' story help us understand the role of women in the tribe of Levi?

4. The collaboration between Miriam and the Egyptian princess to reunite the baby Moses with his mother-turned-wet-nurse crosses ethnic and class lines. Compare and contrast the values of Pharaoh with the values of these women.

The Values of Pharaoh

The Values of These Women

5. The women in this story use their position in society to help Moses, delivering him so that God can use him to deliver the nation. Instead of competing in a man's world, these women worked collaboratively to achieve a goal that wouldn't have been possible for men. Their uniqueness as women gave them access and opportunity that male methods wouldn't have achieved. What unique skill, job, resource, or access might God be calling you to use to aid others? What specific feminine strengths or access do you see in women you admire?

6. A prophetess is a woman who receives a word from the Lord and shares it with another. The visual picture of prophets are those who are filled with the breath and energy of God. Prior to Jesus, prophets functioned like individual spokespeople for limited intervals of time, but now the Holy Spirit breathes his life-giving presence into all Christians.[26] What do you think it looks like today to share a prophecy? If you were to write a song like Miram about what God has done, what would it say?

7. God delivers his people through a number of strategic partnerships between men and women. Name as many partnerships as you can find in this narrative. In what kinds of partnerships do you see God working today?

8. Before they were written down into the original biblical scrolls, the stories in our Bible were part of an oral history. Who but the midwives, Miriam, and Moses' mother could have shared the details about defying Pharaoh's order and rescuing baby Moses? These women not only delivered life, but also testified to what God had done through them.[27] Just like he did with these women, God invites you to share your story. Write down one person you will tell your story to this week.

Lesson 6
Prayer

Sometimes salvation comes with the drama and flourish of parting the Red Sea, but here we see women whose small acts of defiance are no less significant to the outcome of the story. Write a prayer of gratitude for the powerful ways that God has delivered you, great or small.

Rahab

Character Portrait

Who	A prostitute who hid the Israelite spies
When	Late Bronze Age, 1400 BC
Where	Jericho, the first conquered city in the promised land of Canaan

Study Tool

A Broken World — *Understanding God's Judgment*

Movies today have largely shifted away from the "good guys versus bad guys" theme that dominated so much of the cultural tales in our past. More often than not, we learn that evil characters have turned to evil ways because of some harm they endured in their past—a compassionate way to view people that proves realistically accurate in most of those we encounter. Hurt people hurt people, as they say.

The Bible offers a more precise framework for humanity, though, helping us to see that we are all born with a natural bent toward selfish and unwise choices.[28] Trauma may be the catalyst for more egregious evils, but it is only part of the equation. Without God's intervention, we are all destined for judgment because we have all sinned, in ways great and small.

The Bible gives minimal backstory for the nations that oppose Israel, except to say that they are enemies. The various inspired authors, writing to an ancient audience, assume that this is enough information to explain what happens next. As modern readers, we will better understand these stories if we remember a few principles. First, we should notice that God gives his people and the surrounding nations chance after chance to turn from their evil ways. He is remarkably long-suffering. When God does judge an entire people group, we should consider all of the surrounding nations who are now protected from the evil that this group was inflicting. Finally, we must never assume that our modern nations are given the same license for warfare as those we see in the Bible. God's judgment of entire nations in Scripture is constrained to a specific time and place. •

Lesson 7
Passage

God delivers his people from Egypt with a promise to take them to a beautiful and fruitful land—a new kind of Eden—where they can live as his people in peace. Sadly, the Israelites barely shake the Egyptian dust off their sandals before beginning to doubt. For their distrust, the entire generation of refugees must wander in the desert until a new leader, Joshua, is allowed to take them into the Promised Land.

When Culture and Law Collide

In both Canaanite and Israelite culture, we see prostitution recognized as a tolerated, desirable, and yet also stigmatized profession.[29] Biblical law is clear in condemning men who sell their daughters into prostitution, as well as women who elect to participate in it.[30] However, as we saw in the story of Tamar, the social consequences for women who violated this law were regularly more severe than for men. The acceptance of prostitution in ancient cultures helps explain its casual mention in some stories but should not be conflated with God's approval of it.

JOSHUA 2:1-24

[1] Joshua son of Nun secretly sent two men as spies from the Acacia Grove, saying, "Go and scout the land, especially Jericho." So they left, and they came to the house of a prostitute named Rahab, and stayed there.

[2] The king of Jericho was told, "Look, some of the Israelite men have come here tonight to investigate the land." [3] Then the king of Jericho sent word to Rahab and said, "Bring out the men who came to you and entered your house, for they came to investigate the entire land."

[4] But the woman had taken the two men and hidden them. So she said, "Yes, the men did come to me, but I didn't know where they were from. [5] At nightfall, when the city gate was about to close, the men went out, and I don't know where they were going. Chase after them quickly, and you can catch up with them!" [6] But she had taken them up to the roof and hidden them among the stalks of flax that she had arranged on the roof. [7] The men pursued them along the road to the fords of the Jordan, and as soon as they left to pursue them, the city gate was shut.

THE PROMISE TO RAHAB

[8] Before the men fell asleep, she went up on the roof [9] and said to them, "I know that the LORD has given you this land and that the terror of you has fallen on us, and everyone who lives in the land is panicking because of you. [10] For we have heard how the LORD dried up the water of the Red Sea before you when you came out of Egypt, and what you did to Sihon and Og, the two Amorite kings you completely destroyed across the Jordan. [11] When we heard this, we lost heart, and everyone's courage failed because of you, for the LORD your God is God in heaven above and on earth below. [12] Now please swear to me by the LORD that you will also show kindness to my father's family, because I showed kindness to you. Give me a sure sign [13] that you will spare the lives of my father, mother, brothers, sisters, and all who belong to them, and save us from death."

[14] The men answered her, "We will give our lives for yours. If you don't report our mission, we will show kindness and faithfulness to you when the LORD gives us the land."

[15] Then she let them down by a rope through the window, since she lived in a house that was built into the wall of the city. [16] "Go to the hill country so that the men pursuing you won't find you," she said to them. "Hide there for three days until they return; afterward, go on your way."

[17] The men said to her, "We will be free from this oath you made us swear, [18] unless, when we enter the land, you tie this scarlet cord to the window through which you let us down. Bring your father, mother, brothers, and all your father's family into your house. [19] If anyone goes out the doors of your house, his death will be his own fault, and we will be innocent. But if anyone with you in the house should be harmed, his death will be our fault. [20] And if you report our mission, we are free from the oath you made us swear."

²¹ "Let it be as you say," she replied, and she sent them away. After they had gone, she tied the scarlet cord to the window.

²² So the two men went into the hill country and stayed there three days until the pursuers had returned. They searched all along the way, but did not find them. ²³ Then the men returned, came down from the hill country, and crossed the Jordan. They went to Joshua son of Nun and reported everything that had happened to them. ²⁴ They told Joshua, "The LORD has handed over the entire land to us. Everyone who lives in the land is also panicking because of us."

JOSHUA 6:1-25

¹ Now Jericho was strongly fortified because of the Israelites — no one leaving or entering. ² The LORD said to Joshua, "Look, I have handed Jericho, its king, and its best soldiers over to you. ³ March around the city with all the men of war, circling the city one time. Do this for six days. ⁴ Have seven priests carry seven ram's-horn trumpets in front of the ark. But on the seventh day, march around the city seven times, while the priests blow the rams' horns. ⁵ When there is a prolonged blast of the horn and you hear its sound, have all the troops give a mighty shout. Then the city wall will collapse, and the troops will advance, each man straight ahead."

⁶ So Joshua son of Nun summoned the priests and said to them, "Take up the ark of the covenant and have seven priests carry seven rams' horns in front of the ark of the LORD." ⁷ He said to the troops, "Move forward, march around the city, and have the armed men go ahead of the ark of the LORD."

⁸ After Joshua had spoken to the troops, seven priests carrying seven ram's horns before the LORD moved forward and blew the rams' horns; the ark of the LORD's covenant followed them. ⁹ While the rams' horns were blowing, the armed men went in front of the priests who blew the rams' horns, and the rear guard went behind the ark. ¹⁰ But Joshua had commanded the troops, "Do not shout or let your voice be heard. Don't let one word come out of your mouth until the time I say, 'Shout!' Then you are to shout." ¹¹ So the ark of the LORD was carried around the city, circling it once. They returned to the camp and spent the night there.

¹² Joshua got up early the next morning. The priests took the ark of the LORD, ¹³ and the seven priests carrying seven rams' horns marched in front of the ark of the LORD. While the rams' horns were blowing, the armed men went in front of them, and the rear guard went behind the ark of the LORD. ¹⁴ On the second day they marched around the city once and returned to the camp. They did this for six days.

The Oral Tradition of Genealogies

The gospel writer Matthew includes Rahab in the genealogy of Jesus, as the wife of Salma and mother to Boaz, even though this is not specifically mentioned in the Old Testament. Rahab's inclusion in Jesus' lineage must have been an accepted oral tradition during the time of Jesus for her to be included in this way.[31]

¹⁵ Early on the seventh day, they started at dawn and marched around the city seven times in the same way. That was the only day they marched around the city seven times. ¹⁶ After the seventh time, the priests blew the rams' horns, and Joshua said to the troops, "Shout! For the LORD has given you the city. ¹⁷ But the city and everything in it are set apart to the LORD for destruction. Only Rahab the prostitute and everyone with her in the house will live, because she hid the messengers we sent. ¹⁸ But keep yourselves from the things set apart, or you will be set apart for destruction. If you take any of those things, you will set apart the camp of Israel for destruction and make trouble for it. ¹⁹ For all the silver and gold, and the articles of bronze and iron, are dedicated to the LORD and must go into the LORD's treasury."

²⁰ So the troops shouted, and the rams' horns sounded. When they heard the blast of the ram's horn, the troops gave a great shout, and the wall collapsed. The troops advanced into the city, each man straight ahead, and they captured the city. ²¹ They completely destroyed everything in the city with the sword — every man and woman, both young and old, and every ox, sheep, and donkey.

RAHAB AND HER FAMILY SPARED

²² Joshua said to the two men who had scouted the land, "Go to the prostitute's house and bring the woman out of there, and all who are with her, just as you swore to her." ²³ So the young men who had scouted went in and brought out Rahab and her father, mother, brothers, and all who belonged to her. They brought out her whole family and settled them outside the camp of Israel.

²⁴ They burned the city and everything in it, but they put the silver and gold and the articles of bronze and iron into the treasury of the LORD's house. ²⁵ However, Joshua spared Rahab the prostitute, her father's family, and all who belonged to her, because she hid the messengers Joshua had sent to spy on Jericho, and she still lives in Israel today.

Lesson 7 Questions

1. **What similarities in theme or plot structure do you see between the story of Rahab and other women we've studied? How do their stories differ?**

Woman	Compare	Contrast
1.		
2.		
3.		

2. What details does the narrator give about Rahab's household? How does this impact your understanding of her influence and authority?

3. Look at the words that Rahab speaks. What do her words tell us about her understanding of Israel's God? Why does she want to hide the spies?

4. How does Rahab advise the spies? What does this reveal about her position in society?

5. The text does not provide backstory about how Rahab came to her profession. We don't know if she was a willing participant or forced into this lifestyle, but in either case, she would have been on the margins of society. What does this story teach us about how God views women like Rahab?

6. During the final plague in Egypt, the Israelites painted the blood of a spotless lamb over their doorposts so that God's Spirit would pass over their house, sparing their firstborn children and animals from death. This miracle is remembered every year on the feast of Passover. In Rahab's story, we see another passover—a window marked in scarlet that protects a family from God's judgment, simply because they believe. What does it mean to you that God has withheld judgment?

7. God spares Rahab's entire family from the destruction of Jericho, the first exception to the rule God has given about not sparing any enemies,[32] but he doesn't leave her on the fringes of society. She will become one of the matriarchs in the line of Jesus, a mother who shapes the values and character of her family. ⓖ Who in your community is also on the fringes of society? What would it look like to fully welcome them into the family of God? What do they have to offer that you or society might be overlooking?

8. Rahab must wait for the Israelites to rescue her family, but she is no sleepy princess in a tower. How might her action and faith in this story inspire you this week?

Lesson 7
Prayer

Imagine what it must have felt like for Rahab to wait with her family as the Israelite army surrounded Jericho. Share with God what you are waiting on. Pray for his patience as you wait and the ability to trust in his deliverance.

Deborah & Jael

Character Portrait

Deborah	A prophetess and the fourth judge of Israel
Where	Under a date palm tree in the land of Ephraim
Jael	A tent-dwelling woman from the Kenite clan, a descendant of Moses's wife's family
Where	On the plains of Zaanaim
When	Iron Age, 1200–1175 BC

Study Tool

Character Speech — *People and Places*

When women speak in the Bible, they reference people and places that might not sound familiar to us, but would have been rich with meaning for the original readers. If I told you that I flew to DC for a conference last weekend and was wholly unprepared for the weather, you would make a number of inferences just from this single sentence. Most Americans know that "DC" is shorthand for our nation's capital, and you might guess that the conference I attended was connected to politics or government in some way. My comment about the weather would have different meaning if last weekend was February or June and gives you information about where I am flying from.

If I concluded by name dropping my celebrity travel companion, you might imagine me sitting on a very different type of airplane instead of cozying up with a book in coach.

The names of people and places in Deborah's song serve a similar function. Referencing the map on page 73 can help us to visualize the places she mentions, and the family tree on pages 36–37 contains several people whose clans are now participating in the battle Deborah describes. Using these kinds of tools can help us hear the meaning behind references that we might otherwise gloss over or miss. •

Lesson 8
Passage

After the nation of Israel settled in the Promised Land, they were governed by a series of judges. This particularly tumultuous period in the country's history is defined by extreme violence and progressively worse cycles of national rebellion against God's law. The many grievous stories included in the book of Judges demonstrate the horrible effects of sin and how twisted society can become when we do what is right in our own eyes.

JUDGES 4
DEBORAH AND BARAK

1 The Israelites again did what was evil in the sight of the LORD after Ehud had died. 2 So the LORD sold them to King Jabin of Canaan, who reigned in Hazor. The commander of his army was Sisera who lived in Harosheth of the Nations. 3 Then the Israelites cried out to the LORD, because Jabin had nine hundred iron chariots, and he harshly oppressed them twenty years.

4 Deborah, a prophetess and the wife of Lappidoth, was judging Israel at that time. 5 She would sit under the palm tree of Deborah between Ramah and Bethel in the hill country of Ephraim, and the Israelites went up to her to settle disputes.

6 She summoned Barak son of Abinoam from Kedesh in Naphtali and said to him, "Hasn't the LORD, the God of Israel, commanded you, 'Go, deploy the troops on Mount Tabor, and take with you ten thousand men from the Naphtalites and Zebulunites? 7 Then I will lure Sisera commander of Jabin's army, his chariots, and his infantry at the Wadi Kishon to fight against you, and I will hand him over to you.'"

8 Barak said to her, "If you will go with me, I will go. But if you will not go with me, I will not go."

9 "I will gladly go with you," she said, "but you will receive no honor on the road you are about to take, because the LORD will sell Sisera to a woman." So Deborah got up and went with Barak to Kedesh. 10 Barak summoned Zebulun and Naphtali to Kedesh; ten thousand men followed him, and Deborah also went with him.

11 Now Heber the Kenite had moved away from the Kenites, the sons of Hobab, Moses's father-in-law, and pitched his tent beside the oak tree of Zaanannim, which was near Kedesh.

12 It was reported to Sisera that Barak son of Abinoam had gone up Mount Tabor. 13 Sisera summoned all his nine hundred iron chariots and all the troops who were with him from Harosheth of the Nations to the Wadi Kishon. 14 Then Deborah said to Barak, "Go! This is the day the LORD has handed Sisera over to you. Hasn't the LORD gone before you?" So Barak came down from Mount Tabor with ten thousand men following him.

15 The LORD threw Sisera, all his charioteers, and all his army into a panic before Barak's assault. Sisera left his chariot and fled on foot. 16 Barak pursued the chariots and the army as far as Harosheth of the Nations, and the whole army of Sisera fell by the sword; not a single man was left.

17 Meanwhile, Sisera had fled on foot to the tent of Jael, the wife of Heber the Kenite, because there was peace between King Jabin of Hazor and the family of Heber the Kenite. 18 Jael went out to greet Sisera and said to him, "Come in, my LORD. Come in with me. Don't be afraid." So he went into her tent, and she covered him with a blanket. 19 He said to her, "Please give me a little water to drink

for I am thirsty." She opened a container of milk, gave him a drink, and covered him again. ²⁰ Then he said to her, "Stand at the entrance to the tent. If a man comes and asks you, 'Is there a man here?' say, 'No.'" ²¹ While he was sleeping from exhaustion, Heber's wife, Jael, took a tent peg, grabbed a hammer, and went silently to Sisera. She hammered the peg into his temple and drove it into the ground, and he died.

²² When Barak arrived in pursuit of Sisera, Jael went out to greet him and said to him, "Come and I will show you the man you are looking for." So he went in with her, and there was Sisera lying dead with a tent peg through his temple!

²³ That day God subdued King Jabin of Canaan before the Israelites. ²⁴ The power of the Israelites continued to increase against King Jabin of Canaan until they destroyed him.

JUDGES 5

DEBORAH'S SONG

¹ On that day Deborah and Barak son of Abinoam sang:

²When the leaders lead in Israel,
when the people volunteer,
blessed be the LORD.
³ Listen, kings! Pay attention, princes!
I will sing to the LORD;
I will sing praise to the LORD God of Israel.
⁴ LORD, when you came from Seir,
when you marched from the fields of Edom,
the earth trembled,
the skies poured rain,
and the clouds poured water.
⁵ The mountains melted before the LORD,
even Sinai, before the LORD, the God of Israel.

⁶ In the days of Shamgar son of Anath,
in the days of Jael,
the main roads were deserted
because travelers kept to the side roads.
⁷ Villages were deserted,
they were deserted in Israel,
until I, Deborah, arose,
a mother in Israel.
⁸ Israel chose new gods,
then there was war in the city gates.
Not a shield or spear was seen
among forty thousand in Israel.
⁹ My heart is with the leaders of Israel,
with the volunteers of the people.
Blessed be the LORD!
¹⁰ You who ride on white donkeys,

The Poetry of Spoil

Of all people, Sisera's mother encourages the military tradition of taking the women of a defeated army as "spoil." A strong tension appears in this final scene of the song, as we picture her calling out into the night, blissfully unaware of her son's violent defeat.

Meanwhile, Deborah has used extremely powerful and somewhat erotic language to describe Jael's victory. Where the cultural expectation is for men to defeat enemies and carelessly use their women, we instead see Jael, standing powerfully above a now-submissive military leader. The nuances of the Hebrew phrase give the impression of Sisera either dead at Jael's feet or perhaps even on her lap between her legs in a more intimate position. Pierced through by the tent peg, he is dead and also "despoiled." Instead of the Israelite women becoming the spoil of war, Sisera lies ruined as the spoil of Jael.[33]

who sit on saddle blankets,

and who travel on the road, give praise!

¹¹ Let them tell the righteous acts of the LORD,

the righteous deeds of his villagers in Israel,

with the voices of the singers at the watering places.

Then the LORD's people went down to the city gates.

¹² "Awake! Awake, Deborah!

Awake! Awake, sing a song!

Arise, Barak,

and take your prisoners,

son of Abinoam!"

¹³ Then the survivors came down to the nobles;

the LORD's people came down to me against the warriors.

¹⁴ Those with their roots in Amalek came from Ephraim;

Benjamin came with your people after you.

The leaders came down from Machir,

and those who carry a marshal's staff came from Zebulun.

¹⁵ The princes of Issachar were with Deborah;

Issachar was with Barak;

they were under his leadership in the valley.

There was great searching of heart

among the clans of Reuben.

¹⁶ Why did you sit among the sheep pens

listening to the playing of pipes for the flocks?

There was great searching of heart

among the clans of Reuben.

¹⁷ Gilead remained beyond the Jordan.

Dan, why did you linger at the ships?

Asher remained at the seashore

and stayed in his harbors.

¹⁸ The people of Zebulun defied death,

Naphtali also, on the heights of the battlefield.

¹⁹ Kings came and fought.

Then the kings of Canaan fought

at Taanach by the Waters of Megiddo,

but they did not plunder the silver.

²⁰ The stars fought from the heavens;

the stars fought with Sisera from their paths.

²¹ The river Kishon swept them away,

the ancient river, the river Kishon.

March on, my soul, in strength!

²² The horses' hooves then hammered —

the galloping, galloping of his stallions.

²³ "Curse Meroz," says the angel of the LORD,

"Bitterly curse her inhabitants,

for they did not come to help the LORD,

to help the LORD with the warriors."

²⁴ Most blessed of women is Jael,

the wife of Heber the Kenite;

she is most blessed among tent-dwelling women.

²⁵ He asked for water; she gave him milk.

She brought him cream in a majestic bowl·

²⁶ She reached for a tent peg,

her right hand, for a workman's hammer.

Then she hammered Sisera —

she crushed his head;

she shattered and pierced his temple.

²⁷ He collapsed, he fell, he lay down between her feet;

he collapsed, he fell between her feet;

where he collapsed, there he fell — dead.

²⁸ Sisera's mother looked through the window;

she peered through the lattice, crying out:

"Why is his chariot so long in coming?

Why don't I hear the hoofbeats of his horses?"

²⁹ Her wisest princesses answer her;

she even answers herself:

³⁰ "Are they not finding and dividing the spoil —

a girl or two for each warrior,

the spoil of colored garments for Sisera,

the spoil of an embroidered garment or two for my neck?"

³¹ LORD, may all your enemies perish as Sisera did.

But may those who love him

be like the rising of the sun in its strength.

And the land had peace for forty years.

Map of the Canaanite Region

This map shows the approximate allotments given to the 12 tribes when they moved into the promised land. Later during the period of the monarchy, the Philistine states would encroach upon some of the coastline, taking land that once belonged to the tribe of Judah.

ARAM

ASHER

NAPHTALI

Sea of Galilee

MANASSEH

ZEBULUN

Nazareth

Megiddo

ISSACHAR

Taanach

MANASSEH

EPHRAIM

GAD

Great Sea

DAN

BENJAMIN

AMMON

Jerusalem

Bethlehem

Bethany

PHILISTINE STATES

REUBEN

JUDAH

Dead Sea

SIMEON

MOAB

EDOM

Mount Seir

The Ancient Near East

Great Sea

MOAB

EGYPT

EDOM

Mt. Seir

SINAI (THE WILDERNESS OF EGYPT)

ARABIA

Red Sea

Lesson 8 Questions

1. We see several key players in this story. Use the chart below to track the important details:

	Deborah	Barak	Jael	Nation of Israel
What the person does				
What the person says				
How the author describes them/their actions				

2. Now consider how God drives the action of the story. What key words and phrases describe what God does?

3. Using the family tree on pages 36–37 and the map on page 73, circle any of the names in Deborah's song that you recognize. Whose family is she describing?

4. Deborah and Barak's song retells the prose story in poetic form, adding value judgements that are meant to guide our understanding of the narrative. How does Deborah describe God's intervention in the life of his people? How has God intervened in your own life?

5. Look at the two sections that describe Jael's military defeat, considering carefully the details of the narrative and the descriptive words in the poem. What visual images does this language invoke? Where else have you read about "crushing his head"?

6. Jael is a member of the Kenite tribe, a clan of outsiders who are both related to Israel through Moses's in-laws and also possibly their enemies.[34] In what ways is Jael an unexpected conqueror? How does she use her unique position, not as a liability, but as an asset?

7. Think about your own gifts and personal traits. What might others see as a liability that God sees as strength?

8. **Deborah describes herself as "a mother in Israel" and Jael as "most blessed of women" even though the story does not give us many details about their actual families or personal lives. In what ways do these women align with your idea of a good mother or woman? In what ways do they challenge your thinking?**

Lesson 8
Prayer

Marriage and family language is an important thematic element throughout the Bible, used to describe how we relate to God and to other people. Being a mother had such significant cultural importance ❹ that the term was also bestowed upon women in the community as a title of honor, as in Deborah's case, to describe the meaningful impact of their leadership. New Testament writers encourage the church to treat older women as mothers[35] and for these women to train up the next generation in godly living.[36] Considering both the biological and spiritual ways that God might be inviting you to mother, write down the names of three people you feel called to invest in. Pray for them now and ask God to show you ways that you can support and encourage them in the coming weeks.

Naomi & Ruth, Part 1

Character Portrait

Naomi	An elderly woman from Bethlehem who has lost her husband and two sons
Ruth	A Moabite woman, descendent of Abraham's nephew Lot
When	Iron Age, 1100–1050 BC
Where	Territories of Moab and Bethlehem

Study Tool

Divine Authorship — *God Speaks Directly to Us*

In our study questions so far, we have asked what a given part of the story reveals about God's character. We want to guide our reflections back to the nature of God because that's the whole point of the Bible—God is telling us the history of his people so that we will understand what he is like. While we discuss how the human writers of the Bible arrange the story, we must also remember that God is the ultimate author of Scripture. Just as God breathed creation into existence, his Spirit filled the hearts and minds of the human authors who ultimately wrote it all down.[37]

The Bible's authorship makes it different from other literature we read. Because these stories are inspired by God, we should try to avoid reading our own perspective or opinions into the story, but instead look carefully for what God is communicating to us through his Word.[38] ●

Lesson 9 Passage

After Deborah, Jael, and Barak defeat the Canaanites, Israel enjoys forty years of peace until another cycle of violence begins. God continues to raise up new judges, while the people continue to live according to their own flawed ideas about good and evil. In the midst of these cycles of national unfaithfulness, we zoom in for a look at one family who still remembers God's promise to Abraham and Sarah.

RUTH 1

NAOMI'S FAMILY IN MOAB

¹ During the time of the judges, there was a famine in the land. A man left Bethlehem in Judah with his wife and two sons to stay in the territory of Moab for a while. ² The man's name was Elimelech, and his wife's name was Naomi. The names of his two sons were Mahlon and Chilion. They were Ephrathites from Bethlehem in Judah. They entered the fields of Moab and settled there. ³ Naomi's husband, Elimelech, died, and she was left with her two sons. ⁴ Her sons took Moabite women as their wives: one was named Orpah and the second was named Ruth. After they lived in Moab about ten years, ⁵ both Mahlon and Chilion also died, and the woman was left without her two children and without her husband.

RUTH'S LOYALTY TO NAOMI

⁶ She and her daughters-in-law set out to return from the territory of Moab, because she had heard in Moab that the LORD had paid attention to his people's need by providing them food. ⁷ She left the place where she had been living, accompanied by her two daughters-in-law, and traveled along the road leading back to the land of Judah.

⁸ Naomi said to them, "Each of you go back to your mother's home. May the LORD show kindness to you as you have shown to the dead and to me. ⁹ May the LORD grant each of you rest in the house of a new husband." She kissed them, and they wept loudly.

¹⁰ They said to her, "We insist on returning with you to your people."

¹¹ But Naomi replied, "Return home, my daughters. Why do you want to go with me? Am I able to have any more sons who could become your husbands? ¹² Return home, my daughters. Go on, for I am too old to have another husband. Even if I thought there was still hope for me to have a husband tonight and to bear sons, ¹³ would you be willing to wait for them to grow up? Would you restrain yourselves from remarrying? No, my daughters, my life is much too bitter for you to share, because the LORD's hand has turned against me." ¹⁴ Again they wept loudly, and Orpah kissed her mother-in-law, but Ruth clung to her. ¹⁵ Naomi said, "Look, your sister-in-law has gone back to her people and to her gods. Follow your sister-in-law."

¹⁶ But Ruth replied:

> Don't plead with me to abandon you
> or to return and not follow you.
> For wherever you go, I will go,
> and wherever you live, I will live;
> your people will be my people,
> and your God will be my God.
> ¹⁷ Where you die, I will die,
> and there I will be buried.
> May the LORD punish me,
> and do so severely,
> if anything but death separates you
> and me.

¹⁸ When Naomi saw that Ruth was determined to go with her, she stopped talking to her.

¹⁹ The two of them traveled until they came to Bethlehem. When they entered Bethlehem, the whole town was excited about their arrival and the local women exclaimed, "Can this be Naomi?"

²⁰ "Don't call me Naomi. Call me Mara," she answered, "for the Almighty has made me very bitter. ²¹ I went away full, but the LORD has brought me back empty. Why do you call me Naomi, since the LORD has opposed me, and the Almighty has afflicted me?"

²² So Naomi came back from the territory of Moab with her daughter-in-law Ruth the Moabitess. They arrived in Bethlehem at the beginning of the barley harvest.

RUTH 2

RUTH AND BOAZ MEET

¹ Now Naomi had a relative on her husband's side. He was a prominent man of noble character from Elimelech's family. His name was Boaz.

² Ruth the Moabitess asked Naomi, "Will you let me go into the fields and gather fallen grain behind someone with whom I find favor?"

Naomi answered her, "Go ahead, my daughter." ³ So Ruth left and entered the field to gather grain behind the harvesters. She happened to be in the portion of the field belonging to Boaz, who was from Elimelech's family.

⁴ Later, when Boaz arrived from Bethlehem, he said to the harvesters, "The LORD be with you."

"The LORD bless you," they replied.

⁵ Boaz asked his servant who was in charge of the harvesters, "Whose young woman is this?"

⁶ The servant answered, "She is the young Moabite woman who returned with Naomi from the territory of Moab. ⁷ She asked, 'Will you let me gather fallen grain among the bundles behind the harvesters?' She came and has been on her feet since early morning, except that she rested a little in the shelter."

⁸ Then Boaz said to Ruth, "Listen, my daughter. Don't go and gather grain in another field, and don't leave this one, but stay here close to my female servants. ⁹ See which field they are harvesting, and follow them. Haven't I ordered the young men not to touch you? When you are thirsty, go and drink from the jars the young men have filled."

¹⁰ She fell facedown, bowed to the ground, and said to him, "Why have I found favor with you, so that you notice me, although I am a foreigner?"

¹¹ Boaz answered her, "Everything you have done for your mother-in-law since your husband's death has been fully reported to me: how you left your father and mother and your native land, and how you came to a people you didn't previously know. ¹² May the LORD reward you for what you have done, and may you receive a full reward from the LORD God of Israel, under whose wings you have come for refuge."

¹³ "My Lord," she said, "I have found favor with you, for you have comforted and encouraged your servant, although I am not like one of your female servants."

¹⁴ At mealtime Boaz told her, "Come over here and have some bread and dip it in the vinegar sauce." So she sat beside the harvesters, and he offered her roasted grain. She ate and was satisfied and had some left over.

¹⁵ When she got up to gather grain, Boaz ordered his young men, "Let her even gather grain among the bundles, and don't humiliate her. ¹⁶ Pull out some stalks from the bundles for her and leave them for her to gather. Don't rebuke her." ¹⁷ So Ruth gathered grain in the field until evening. She beat out what she had gathered, and it was about twenty-six quarts of barley. ¹⁸ She picked up the grain and went into the town, where her mother-in-law saw what she had gleaned. She brought out what she had left over from her meal and gave it to her.

¹⁹ Her mother-in-law said to her, "Where did you gather barley today, and where did you work? May the LORD bless the man who noticed you."

Ruth told her mother-in-law whom she had worked with and said, "The name of the man I worked with today is Boaz."

²⁰ Then Naomi said to her daughter-in-law, "May the LORD bless him because he has not abandoned his kindness to the living or the dead." Naomi continued, "The man is a close relative. He is one of our family redeemers."

²¹ Ruth the Moabitess said, "He also told me, 'Stay with my young men until they have finished all of my harvest.'"

²² So Naomi said to her daughter-in-law Ruth, "My daughter, it is good for you to work with his female servants, so that nothing will happen to you in another field." ²³ Ruth stayed close to Boaz's female servants and gathered grain until the barley and the wheat harvests were finished. And she lived with her mother-in-law.

Lesson 9 Questions

1. The book of Ruth is set during the same tumultuous period as the book of Judges. List five differences you notice between the opening of this story and that of Deborah and Jael.

2. Considering what you know about household structures ❶ and work, ❺ what challenges might Naomi and her daughters-in-law have faced?

3. Ruth's story is rich with detail about the main characters. How is each described by the author? What do you observe about their values?

Naomi	Ruth	Boaz

4. What is Naomi's complaint and against whom? How does her language impact your understanding of prayer?

5. List the ways that Boaz protects Ruth. How does this protection echo God's protection of his people? How does it echo God's protection of you?

6. Even in such a tumultuous period of Israel's history, Ruth and Naomi are an example of an individual family of faith that sustained their allegiance to God. What does including this private, personal story show us about God's geopolitical priorities? How might their story provide comfort for us today?

7. **Remember the promise that God made to Abraham and Sarah about their descendants? God recommits his covenant with Moses, promising to be loyal to Israel and asking them for loyalty in return. In what ways does Ruth's loyalty reflect God's loyalty?**

8. We've read about the obligation of a family redeemer before. Given what happened to Tamar, what might you expect to happen to Ruth? What reasons might Ruth still have for hope?

Lesson 9
Prayer

Naomi and Ruth are a beautiful example of faithfulness, humility, and strength. Write a prayer of thanksgiving for women you know who exemplify godly living. List out specific traits you admire and praise God for his work in their lives.

Naomi & Ruth, Part 2

Character Portrait

Naomi	An elderly woman from Bethlehem who has lost her husband and two sons
Ruth	A Moabite woman, descendent of Abraham's nephew Lot
When	Iron Age, 1100–1050 BC
Where	Territories of Moab and Bethlehem

Study Tool

Character Speech — *A Chorus of Voices*

Many ancient texts focus on formal regulations and public positions within a society, which can skew our understanding of just how patriarchal a community would have felt to its citizens.[39] The book of Ruth gives generous attention to the perspectives and voices of women, allowing us a peek into their day-to-day experiences. By taking time to listen to women's stories in the Bible, we can see their essential involvement in God's story, despite the stereotypes of the day. •

Lesson 10
Passage

¹ Ruth's mother-in-law Naomi said to her, "My daughter, shouldn't I find rest for you, so that you will be taken care of? ² Now isn't Boaz our relative? Haven't you been working with his female servants? This evening he will be winnowing barley on the threshing floor. ³ Wash, put on perfumed oil, and wear your best clothes. Go down to the threshing floor, but don't let the man know you are there until he has finished eating and drinking. ⁴ When he lies down, notice the place where he's lying, go in and uncover his feet, and lie down. Then he will explain to you what you should do."

⁵ So Ruth said to her, "I will do everything you say." ⁶ She went down to the threshing floor and did everything her mother-in-law had charged her to do. ⁷ After Boaz ate, drank, and was in good spirits, he went to lie down at the end of the pile of barley, and she came secretly, uncovered his feet, and lay down.

⁸ At midnight, Boaz was startled, turned over, and there lying at his feet was a woman! ⁹ So he asked, "Who are you?"

"I am Ruth, your servant," she replied. "Take me under your wing, for you are a family redeemer."

¹⁰ Then he said, "May the LORD bless you, my daughter. You have shown more kindness now than before, because you have not pursued younger men, whether rich or poor. ¹¹ Now don't be afraid, my daughter. I will do for you whatever you say, since all the people in my town know that you are a woman of noble character. ¹² Yes, it is true that I am a family redeemer, but there is a redeemer closer than I am. ¹³ Stay here tonight, and in the morning, if he wants to redeem you, that's good. Let him redeem you. But if he doesn't want to redeem you, as the LORD lives, I will. Now lie down until morning."

¹⁴ So she lay down at his feet until morning but got up while it was still dark. Then Boaz said, "Don't let it be known that a woman came to the threshing floor." ¹⁵ And he told Ruth, "Bring the shawl you're wearing and hold it out." When she held it out, he shoveled six measures of barley into her shawl, and she went into the town.

¹⁶ She went to her mother-in-law, Naomi, who asked her, "What happened, my daughter?"

Then Ruth told her everything the man had done for her. ¹⁷ She said, "He gave me these six measures of barley, because he said, 'Don't go back to your mother-in-law empty-handed.'"

¹⁸ Naomi said, "My daughter, wait until you find out how things go, for he won't rest unless he resolves this today."

What did Boaz know?

We can tell from Boaz's response to Ruth that he is well aware of her situation. Bethlehem is a small village, so when the women returned, it would not have taken long for everyone in town to know that Elimelech's widow and daughter-in-law had come back home. Boaz knows that he's the second redeemer in line, responsible for taking care of Ruth and Naomi, and yet he has not proactively taken any action to encourage the other redeemer toward marriage. Ruth's prompting reminds him to do the right thing, initiating a partnership that will restore their family line.

RUTH 4

RUTH AND BOAZ MARRY

¹ Boaz went to the gate of the town and sat down there. Soon the family redeemer Boaz had spoken about came by. Boaz said, "Come over here and sit down." So he went over and sat down.

² Then Boaz took ten men of the town's elders and said, "Sit here." And they sat down. ³ He said to the redeemer, "Naomi, who has returned from the territory of Moab, is selling the portion of the field that belonged to our brother Elimelech. ⁴ I thought I should inform you: Buy it back in the presence of those seated here and in the presence of the elders of my people. If you want to redeem it, do it. But if you do not want to redeem it, tell me so that I will know, because there isn't anyone other than you to redeem it, and I am next after you."

"I want to redeem it," he answered.

⁵ Then Boaz said, "On the day you buy the field from Naomi, you will acquire Ruth the Moabitess, the wife of the deceased man, to perpetuate the man's name on his property."

⁶ The redeemer replied, "I can't redeem it myself, or I will ruin my own inheritance. Take my right of redemption, because I can't redeem it."

⁷ At an earlier period in Israel, a man removed his sandal and gave it to the other party in order to make any matter legally binding concerning the right of redemption or the exchange of property. This was the method of legally binding a transaction in Israel.

⁸ So the redeemer removed his sandal and said to Boaz, "Buy back the property yourself."

⁹ Boaz said to the elders and all the people, "You are witnesses today that I am buying from Naomi everything that belonged to Elimelech, Chilion, and Mahlon. ¹⁰ I have also acquired Ruth the Moabitess, Mahlon's widow, as my wife, to perpetuate the deceased man's name on his property, so that his name will not disappear among his relatives or from the gate of his hometown. You are witnesses today."

¹¹ All the people who were at the city gate, including the elders, said, "We are witnesses. May the LORD make the woman who is entering your house like Rachel and Leah, who together built the house of Israel. May you be powerful in Ephrathah and your name well known in Bethlehem. ¹² May your house become like the house of Perez, the son Tamar bore to Judah, because of the offspring the LORD will give you by this young woman."

¹³ Boaz took Ruth and she became his wife. He slept with her, and the LORD granted conception to her, and she gave birth to a son. ¹⁴ The women said to Naomi, "Blessed be the LORD, who has not left you without a family redeemer today. May his name become well known in Israel. ¹⁵ He will renew your life and sustain you in your old age. Indeed, your daughter-in-law, who loves you and is better to you than seven sons, has given birth to him." ¹⁶ Naomi took the child, placed him on her lap, and became a mother to him. ¹⁷ The neighbor women said, "A son has been born to Naomi," and they named him Obed. He was the father of Jesse, the father of David.

DAVID'S GENEALOGY FROM JUDAH'S SON

¹⁸ Now these are the family records of Perez:

> Perez fathered Hezron,
> ¹⁹ Hezron fathered Ram,
> Ram fathered Amminadab,
> ²⁰ Amminadab fathered Nahshon,
> Nahshon fathered Salmon,
> ²¹ Salmon fathered Boaz,
> Boaz fathered Obed,
> ²² Obed fathered Jesse,
> and Jesse fathered David.

Lesson 10 Questions

1. **Ruth and Naomi craft a very practical plan for how to approach Boaz privately in the night, uncovering his feet so that he would wake naturally when his feet got cold.[40] What did Naomi recommend for Ruth to do? What actions did Ruth add to the plan?**

2. List all the phrases that are used to honor Ruth in this section. How do these traits inform your understanding of godliness?

3. The other redeemer seems interested in Naomi's property until he learns that he would potentially drain his resources to provide an heir for Mahlon. Do you expect God's attitude toward redemption to be more like this redeemer or like Boaz? Explain what you mean.

4. Consider what you observed about Naomi's complaint compared to the women's praise at the resolution of the story. What has God done for Naomi?

5. The women make a hopeful comparison between Ruth and Tamar. How are their stories similar? How do they differ?

6. Ruth and Naomi's story explores the themes of emptiness and fullness,[41] opening with three women who have empty wombs, empty marriage beds, and are left alone without protection. List other references you find to emptiness and fullness. Who does the story credit for filling them up? How do the themes of emptiness and fullness relate in your own life right now?

7. Ruth's need for a redeemer parallels Israel's need for redemption, both of which will come at a cost. What is God willing to pay to redeem his people? Push past the simple answer to meditate on the specifics. See if you can name five.

8. Naomi and Ruth, like many of the women we have studied, don't conform to stereotypes nor are they preoccupied with flouting the status quo.[42] They don't have anything to prove. In what ways does their example free you from the cultural expectations for women today?

Lesson 10
Prayer

Ruth takes responsibility for the protection and provision of Naomi,[43] and ultimately Boaz also fully provides for both women. Write a prayer of thanksgiving for those who offer you protection and provision. Confess any ways you might be avoiding your own responsibilities. Ask God for the strength you need to course-correct.

Thematic Recap

Part Two brought us through the Red Sea and into the wilderness, with new landscapes and new perspectives. Flip back through the women we met in this part of the biblical narrative and consider these and other themes that stood out to you. What ideas about God, womanhood, and yourself were most impactful for you?

About God	About Womanhood	About Myself
Remains loyal to his promises	Powerful community influencers	
Teams up with unexpected women	Rejecting stereotypes	
Speaks to us directly	Active participants	
Welcomes the sojourner	Faithfulness to God	
Values the voices of women	Uniquely feminine strengths	

Interlude: *Our Welcoming God*

I know that spring is finally here in Los Angeles when I am greeted by the smell of jasmine on the landing below my office. May is jacaranda season, which explodes in plumes of purple along the city streets. Summer is actually in October; it comes at the precise moment when I think, *I guess this year was not so bad without air conditioning.* That's when the heat rolls in, and I roll my sweaters neatly once again at the back of their drawers for a few more weeks.

After nearly a decade, I finally understand the whims of this strange and beautiful city that I call home. I'm not a native Californian, but I've been here long enough to feel like I don't quite belong back in Texas either. Like the women we've been studying, I'm a bit of a wanderer, a sojourner in a new land where God called me to go.

The years that Israel spent in the desert must have been a wild ride. Children's stories left me with the impression that this grumbling group of people trudged around aimlessly for a generation. It sounded very boring. And then, when they got into the Promised Land, it was just a lot of genealogies and rules and wars with people groups that don't mean much to our modern ear. I guess this is why we often skip over some of these sections in our Bible.

But there is a part of Exodus that I finally started to understand in recent years. The instructions for the tabernacle are more than construction plans with foreign weights and measures—they have a theological purpose. God is designing a way to dwell among his people. He is sharing as much of himself as he safely can in a carefully arranged structure with curtains like shades of specialized glasses used to look at the sun. We who are tainted by sin cannot get back to God's presence, so he will draw near to us.

To create this beautiful connection point, God invites tapestry weavers, goldsmiths, and embroiderers to share their talent and fill the space with rich, visual reminders of the paradise we lost and the one that is yet to come.

The design for the tabernacle is repeated in a permanent temple in Jerusalem, which would be destroyed and rebuilt decades after Israel's kingdom fell. In this second temple, the very priests who conspire against Jesus enjoy access to God's presence—that is, until Christ's crucifixion shakes the earth and tears the protective curtain between the people and the temple's holiest place. The design for the temple was perfected in the body of Christ, a temple destroyed and rebuilt eternally in our hearts. We no longer need to be protected from his perfect holiness. With our sin soaked up by the atoning blood of Jesus, we are made clean. We are no longer restricted from holy ground. He has come to dwell with us.

My holy ground is a patch of sand along the Pacific Ocean. It's not the sand that is special, nor the ocean, but rather the sense of awe I find in softly roaring waves and endless horizon. I feel God's presence in the sea—so powerful it could swallow me up, and yet so inviting and fresh, with its gentle spray on my skin and wind-swept hair. When I look out into the ocean, I think of Jesus telling his disciples about the place he has prepared, his Father's house with many rooms. God welcomes us into his presence now, and one day, when the wanderings cease, we will enjoy our permanent home with him.

I do love my city, but it isn't my home.

Home isn't a studio on Santa Monica Boulevard any more than a 3-bed/2-bath in Crenshaw. It's not a ranch or a high rise or a bungalow or a tent. Here on earth, my home will always be in the presence of my Lord, whether I am meeting with him on a sunny beach or in the security of a tear-soaked shower. We find rest for our weary souls with the one who incessantly pursues us in the wilderness. And there, he prepares a banqueting table for us under the banner of love. •

PART THREE

The Rulers

*God keeps choosing people on the **fringes of society** to do his work.*

LESSON 11

Hannah

Character Portrait

Who	The barren wife of Elkanah, a descendent of Joseph
When	Iron Age, 1100–1075 BC
Where	The hill country of Ephraim and the city of Shiloh

Study Tool

Patterns — God's Unexpected Choices

The beginning of 1 Samuel follows a pattern that we have seen before. History books may begin with kings and rulers, panning across the battlefield or zooming out from important treaties, but the narratives of the Bible often begin in quiet, domestic spaces,[44] with midwives or in the midst of difficult family tragedies. The original readers expected the firstborn, the strong, and the beautiful to be victorious. Often we do, too. But God keeps choosing people on the fringes of society to do his work. "Humans do not see what the Lord sees, for humans see what is visible, but the Lord sees the heart."[45] The patterns that God establishes in Scripture not only tell us what he is like but foreshadow the grand plan he has in store for all of us. •

Lesson 11
Passage

Hannah's story is the opening act for the Kingdom period of the nation of Israel. At the end of the exhausting cycle of judges, where violence seems to be the only constant, we meet another man with two warring wives. The first wife has an empty womb, but her spirit-filled heart will change the course of the nation of Israel.

1 SAMUEL 1

[1] There was a man from Ramathaim-zophim in the hill country of Ephraim. His name was Elkanah son of Jeroham, son of Elihu, son of Tohu, son of Zuph, an Ephraimite. [2] He had two wives, the first named Hannah and the second Peninnah. Peninnah had children, but Hannah was childless. [3] This man would go up from his town every year to worship and to sacrifice to the Lord of Armies at Shiloh, where Eli's two sons, Hophni and Phinehas, were the Lord's priests.

[4] Whenever Elkanah offered a sacrifice, he always gave portions of the meat to his wife Peninnah and to each of her sons and daughters. [5] But he gave a double portion to Hannah, for he loved her even though the Lord had kept her from conceiving. [6] Her rival would taunt her severely just to provoke her, because the Lord had kept Hannah from conceiving. [7] Year after year, when she went up to the Lord's house, her rival taunted her in this way. Hannah would weep and would not eat. [8] "Hannah, why are you crying?" her husband, Elkanah, would ask. "Why won't you eat? Why are you troubled? Am I not better to you than ten sons?"

[9] On one occasion, Hannah got up after they ate and drank at Shiloh. The priest Eli was sitting on a chair by the doorpost of the Lord's temple. [10] Deeply hurt, Hannah prayed to the Lord and wept with many tears. [11] Making a vow, she pleaded, "Lord of Armies, if you will take notice of your servant's affliction, remember and not forget me, and give your servant a son, I will give him to the Lord all the days of his life, and his hair will never be cut."

[12] While she continued praying in the Lord's presence, Eli watched her mouth. [13] Hannah was praying silently, and though her lips were moving, her voice could not be heard. Eli thought she was drunk [14] and said to her, "How long are you going to be drunk? Get rid of your wine!"

[15] "No, my lord," Hannah replied. "I am a woman with a broken heart. I haven't had any wine or beer; I've been pouring out my heart before the Lord. [16] Don't think of me as a wicked woman; I've been praying from the depth of my anguish and resentment."

[17] Eli responded, "Go in peace, and may the God of Israel grant the request you've made of him."

[18] "May your servant find favor with you," she replied. Then Hannah went on her way; she ate and no longer looked despondent.

SAMUEL'S BIRTH AND DEDICATION

[19] The next morning Elkanah and Hannah got up early to worship before the Lord. Afterward, they returned home to Ramah. Then Elkanah was intimate with his wife Hannah, and the Lord remembered her. [20] After some time, Hannah conceived and gave birth to a son. She named him Samuel, because she said, "I requested him from the Lord."

²¹ When Elkanah and all his household went up to make the annual sacrifice and his vow offering to the LORD, ²² Hannah did not go and explained to her husband, "After the child is weaned, I'll take him to appear in the LORD's presence and to stay there permanently."

²³ Her husband, Elkanah, replied, "Do what you think is best, and stay here until you've weaned him. May the LORD confirm your word." So Hannah stayed there and nursed her son until she weaned him. ²⁴ When she had weaned him, she took him with her to Shiloh, as well as a three-year-old bull, half a bushel of flour, and a clay jar of wine. Though the boy was still young, she took him to the LORD's house at Shiloh. ²⁵ Then they slaughtered the bull and brought the boy to Eli.

²⁶ "Please, my lord," she said, "as surely as you live, my lord, I am the woman who stood here beside you praying to the LORD. ²⁷ I prayed for this boy, and since the LORD gave me what I asked him for, ²⁸ I now give the boy to the LORD. For as long as he lives, he is given to the LORD." Then he worshiped the LORD there.

1 SAMUEL 2
HANNAH'S TRIUMPHANT PRAYER

¹ Hannah prayed:

> My heart rejoices in the LORD;
> my horn is lifted up by the LORD.
> My mouth boasts over my enemies,
> because I rejoice in your salvation.
> ² There is no one holy like the LORD.
> There is no one besides you!
> And there is no rock like our God.
> ³ Do not boast so proudly,
> or let arrogant words come out of your mouth,
> for the LORD is a God of knowledge,
> and actions are weighed by him.
> ⁴ The bows of the warriors are broken,
> but the feeble are clothed with strength.
> ⁵ Those who are full hire themselves out for food,
> but those who are starving hunger no more.
> The woman who is childless gives birth to seven,
> but the woman with many sons pines away.
> ⁶ The LORD brings death and gives life;
> he sends some down to Sheol, and he raises others up.
> ⁷ The LORD brings poverty and gives wealth;
> he humbles and he exalts.
> ⁸ He raises the poor from the dust
> and lifts the needy from the trash heap.
> He seats them with noblemen

Hannah's Vow

Hannah makes a Nazirite vow, which is a special dedication to service of the Lord that includes abstaining from wine and not cutting one's hair.[46] Two other significant Nazirites in the Bible are Samson and John the Baptist.

By dedicating Samuel to serve the Lord in this way, Hannah commits to sending him to live at the temple where the priests would raise and train him. Samuel embraces the vow of his mother and grows up to be a faithful and wise man. He was the first since Moses to receive direct communication from the Lord and spoke many prophecies to the people of Israel. He was also a high priest and the final judge before the Israelite monarchy was established. Although imperfect, Samuel remained committed to serving the Lord until the day he died.

and gives them a throne of honor.
For the foundations of the earth are the LORD's;
he has set the world on them.
⁹ He guards the steps of his faithful ones,
but the wicked perish in darkness,
for a person does not prevail by his own strength.
¹⁰ Those who oppose the LORD will be shattered;
he will thunder in the heavens against them.
The LORD will judge the ends of the earth.
He will give power to his king;
he will lift up the horn of his anointed.

¹¹ Elkanah went home to Ramah, but the boy served the LORD in the presence of the priest Eli.

ELI'S FAMILY JUDGED

¹² Eli's sons were wicked men; they did not respect the LORD ¹³ or the priests' share of the sacrifices from the people. When anyone offered a sacrifice, the priest's servant would come with a three-pronged meat fork while the meat was boiling ¹⁴ and plunge it into the container, kettle, cauldron, or cooking pot. The priest would claim for himself whatever the meat fork brought up. This is the way they treated all the Israelites who came there to Shiloh. ¹⁵ Even before the fat was burned, the priest's servant would come and say to the one who was sacrificing, "Give the priest some meat to roast, because he won't accept boiled meat from you — only raw." ¹⁶ If that person said to him, "The fat must be burned first; then you can take whatever you want for yourself," the servant would reply, "No, I insist that you hand it over right now. If you don't, I'll take it by force!" ¹⁷ So the servants' sin was very severe in the presence of the LORD, because the men treated the LORD's offering with contempt.

¹⁸ Samuel served in the LORD's presence —this mere boy was dressed in the linen ephod. ¹⁹ Each year his mother made him a little robe and took it to him when she went with her husband to offer the annual sacrifice. ²⁰ Eli would bless Elkanah and his wife: "May the LORD give you children by this woman in place of the one she has given to the LORD." Then they would go home.

²¹ The LORD paid attention to Hannah's need, and she conceived and gave birth to three sons and two daughters. Meanwhile, the boy Samuel grew up in the presence of the LORD.

²² Now Eli was very old. He heard about everything his sons were doing to all Israel and how they were sleeping with the women who served at the entrance to the tent of meeting. ²³ He said to them, "Why are you doing these things? I have heard about your evil actions from all these people. ²⁴ No, my sons, the news I hear the LORD's people spreading is not good. ²⁵ If one person sins against another, God can intercede for him, but if a person sins against the LORD, who can intercede for him?" But they would not listen to their father, since the LORD intended to kill them. ²⁶ By contrast, the boy Samuel grew in stature and in favor with the LORD and with people.

[27] A man of God came to Eli and said to him, "This is what the Lord says: 'Didn't I reveal myself to your forefather's family when they were in Egypt and belonged to Pharaoh's palace? [28] Out of all the tribes of Israel, I chose your house to be my priests, to offer sacrifices on my altar, to burn incense, and to wear an ephod in my presence. I also gave your forefather's family all the Israelite food offerings. [29] Why, then, do all of you despise my sacrifices and offerings that I require at the place of worship? You have honored your sons more than me, by making yourselves fat with the best part of all of the offerings of my people Israel.'

[30] "Therefore, this is the declaration of the Lord, the God of Israel: 'I did say that your family and your forefather's family would walk before me forever. But now,' this is the Lord's declaration, 'no longer! For those who honor me I will honor, but those who despise me will be disgraced. [31] Look, the days are coming when I will cut off your strength and the strength of your forefather's family, so that none in your family will reach old age. [32] You will see distress in the place of worship, in spite of all that is good in Israel, and no one in your family will ever again reach old age. [33] Any man from your family I do not cut off from my altar will bring grief and sadness to you. All your descendants will die violently. [34] This will be the sign that will come to you concerning your two sons Hophni and Phinehas: both of them will die on the same day.

[35] "'Then I will raise up a faithful priest for myself. He will do whatever is in my heart and mind. I will establish a lasting dynasty for him, and he will walk before my anointed one for all time. [36] Anyone who is left in your family will come and bow down to him for a piece of silver or a loaf of bread. He will say: Please appoint me to some priestly office so I can have a piece of bread to eat.'"

Lesson 11 Questions

1. Consider Hannah's predicament in light of her position in the family ❸ as well as her potential future after Elkanah dies. ❹ How dire is her situation? What external pressures and motivations might add to the already painful personal experience of infertility?

2. Both Hannah's husband and the priest Eli misunderstand and minimize her grief. What misjudgment does each one make? What do you think God sees?

3. Compare Hannah's devotion to God and what the author tells us about Eli and his sons. How do the sons reflect their father? What might we expect from the son of Hannah?

4. Hannah sojourns with her husband to the temple, making her request for fertility to God instead of seeking other common (and likely tempting) sources of hope ❼ or following in the footsteps of Sarah, Rachel, and Leah. Do you have a similarly urgent desire right now? Where are you turning for power or control?

5. Samuel means "God has heard." Besides her actual request, what else has God heard from Hannah? Take time to consider all the details we have learned in the story. What do you think God hears from you? What do you want him to hear this week?

6. Samuel is likely about 3 years old when Hannah brings him to the temple to begin his life of service with the priesthood. Her parting words are a song of God's faithfulness. How does this song offer hope for Hannah as she leaves her toddler in God's hands? How might these words impact her growing child?

7. After leaving her only child to serve God, the Biblical author tells us that "the LORD paid attention to Hannah's need,"[47] providing her with a large family to enjoy and to care for her in old age. In what ways do you see God taking care of your needs? Share a time when his provision defied your expectations.

8. Hannah's son, Samuel, is the faithful priest that God promises to raise up instead of the house of Eli. Samuel will go on to anoint both King Saul and then King David, providing wisdom for the nation of Israel in its earliest years. What patterns do you see between Hannah's family and the women before her?

Lesson 11
Prayer

Hannah demonstrates a deep theological understanding and giftedness as a poet, and her song is recorded as an example intended to lead all God's people into worship, including us.[48] Pick three statements about God that Hannah includes in her song. Share your reaction to these truths in prayer. Offer thanksgiving. Ask God to help your unbelief. Pray that God would be faithful to his promises.

Abigail

Character Portrait

Who	King David's second wife, rescued from her marriage to the evil Nabal
When	1025–1005 BC
Where	Near Jerusalem

Study Tool

A Broken World — *Unsafe Spaces*

Adam and Eve had a great thing going in Eden. Equally made in the image of God, they shared the blessing of fruitfulness and governance, each bringing their beautifully designed differences to a partnership meant for mutual flourishing. But after they sinned, their broken relationship with God led to broken relationships between men and women on earth. Men used their relative strength and social power not to guard or provide for the women in their care but to dominate them.

In the ancient world this sometimes looked like disregarding women's valuable insights or feelings. It could also be much, much worse. Women's physical safety was often at risk if the men in their lives abdicated responsibility or used them cruelly.

Such oppression was never God's design for his daughters. Provision for women's safety is sprinkled throughout the Mosaic Law and affirmed in the teachings of Jesus. •

Lesson 12
Passage

Hannah's son Samuel anoints Saul, the strong and charismatic descendent of Benjamin, to be the first king of Israel. Saul leads Israel in military victory against the Philistines but eventually turns his heart away from the Lord. Samuel recognizes God's rejection of Saul, anointing David instead as the rightful king. Saul remains in power, while David holds a number of roles in the royal court—a harpist to soothe Saul's bad dreams, the king's armor bearer, best friend to Saul's son Jonathan, and eventually the husband of Saul's daughter Michal. David is finally driven away by Saul's anger, and leads a group of his own soldiers on the run.

Ancient Hospitality

Abigail brings the gift to David that Nabal should have sent. Not only was David's modest request well within the cultural expectations for hospitality toward strangers, but David and his men had kept Nabal's shepherds from harm in the wilderness and deserved at least his kindness if not some kind of repayment.

Hospitality for the Israelites was more than a social nicety or way to show off one's culinary or decorative skills; it was a sacred duty defined in the Law.[49] Throughout the Bible, we see examples of gracious hosts, some who lavishly honor their guests out of their abundance and some who are honored for sacrificing what little they have. In Psalm 23, King David compares God to both a shepherd and host, who provides not only food and drink but protection within his home.[50]

1 SAMUEL 25

DAVID, NABAL, AND ABIGAIL

1 Samuel died, and all Israel assembled to mourn for him, and they buried him by his home in Ramah. David then went down to the Wilderness of Paran.

2 A man in Maon had a business in Carmel; he was a very rich man with three thousand sheep and one thousand goats and was shearing his sheep in Carmel. 3 The man's name was Nabal, and his wife's name, Abigail. The woman was intelligent and beautiful, but the man, a Calebite, was harsh and evil in his dealings.

4 While David was in the wilderness, he heard that Nabal was shearing sheep, 5 so David sent ten young men instructing them, "Go up to Carmel, and when you come to Nabal, greet him in my name. 6 Then say this: 'Long life to you, and peace to you, peace to your family, and peace to all that is yours. 7 I hear that you are shearing. When your shepherds were with us, we did not harass them, and nothing of theirs was missing the whole time they were in Carmel. 8 Ask your young men, and they will tell you. So let my young men find favor with you, for we have come on a feast day. Please give whatever you have on hand to your servants and to your son David.'"

9 David's young men went and said all these things to Nabal on David's behalf, and they waited. 10 Nabal asked them, "Who is David? Who is Jesse's son? Many slaves these days are running away from their masters. 11 Am I supposed to take my bread, my water, and my meat that I butchered for my shearers and give them to these men? I don't know where they are from."

12 David's young men retraced their steps. When they returned to him, they reported all these words. 13 He said to his men, "All of you, put on your swords!" So each man put on his sword, and David also put on his sword. About four hundred men followed David while two hundred stayed with the supplies.

14 One of Nabal's young men informed Abigail, Nabal's wife, "Look, David sent messengers from the wilderness to greet our master, but he screamed at them. 15 The men treated us very well. When we were in the field, we weren't harassed and nothing of ours was missing the whole time we were living among them. 16 They were a wall around us, both day and night, the entire time we were with them herding the sheep. 17 Now consider carefully what you should do, because there is certain to be trouble for our master and his entire family. He is such a worthless fool nobody can talk to him!"

18 Abigail hurried, taking two hundred loaves of bread, two clay jars of wine, five butchered sheep, a bushel of roasted grain, one hundred

clusters of raisins, and two hundred cakes of pressed figs, and loaded them on donkeys. ¹⁹ Then she said to her male servants, "Go ahead of me. I will be right behind you." But she did not tell her husband, Nabal.

²⁰ As she rode the donkey down a mountain pass hidden from view, she saw David and his men coming toward her and met them. ²¹ David had just said, "I guarded everything that belonged to this man in the wilderness for nothing. He was not missing anything, yet he paid me back evil for good. ²² May God punish me and do so severely if I let any of his males survive until morning."

²³ When Abigail saw David, she quickly got off the donkey and knelt down with her face to the ground and paid homage to David. ²⁴ She knelt at his feet and said, "The guilt is mine, my lord, but please let your servant speak to you directly. Listen to the words of your servant. ²⁵ My lord should pay no attention to this worthless fool Nabal, for he lives up to his name: His name means 'stupid,' and stupidity is all he knows. I, your servant, didn't see my lord's young men whom you sent. ²⁶ Now my lord, as surely as the LORD lives and as you yourself live— it is the LORD who kept you from participating in bloodshed and avenging yourself by your own hand—may your enemies and those who intend to harm my lord be like Nabal. ²⁷ Let this gift your servant has brought to my lord be given to the young men who follow my lord. ²⁸ Please forgive your servant's offense, for the LORD is certain to make a lasting dynasty for my lord because he fights the LORD's battles. Throughout your life, may evil not be found in you.

²⁹ "Someone is pursuing you and intends to take your life. My lord's life is tucked safely in the place where the LORD your God protects the living, but he is flinging away your enemies' lives like stones from a sling. ³⁰ When the LORD does for my lord all the good he promised you and appoints you ruler over Israel, ³¹ there will not be remorse or a troubled conscience for my lord because of needless bloodshed or my lord's revenge. And when the LORD does good things for my lord, may you remember me your servant."

³² Then David said to Abigail, "Blessed be the LORD God of Israel, who sent you to meet me today! ³³ May your discernment be blessed, and may you be blessed. Today you kept me from participating in bloodshed and avenging myself by my own hand. ³⁴ Otherwise, as surely as the LORD God of Israel lives, who prevented me from harming you, if you had not come quickly to meet me, Nabal wouldn't have had any males left by morning light." ³⁵ Then David accepted what she had brought him and said,

"Go home in peace. See, I have heard what you said and have granted your request."

³⁶ Then Abigail went to Nabal, and there he was in his house, holding a feast fit for a king. Nabal's heart was cheerful, and he was very drunk, so she didn't say anything to him until morning light.

³⁷ In the morning when Nabal sobered up, his wife told him about these events. His heart died and he became a stone. ³⁸ About ten days later, the LORD struck Nabal dead.

³⁹ When David heard that Nabal was dead, he said, "Blessed be the LORD who championed my cause against Nabal's insults and restrained his servant from doing evil. The LORD brought Nabal's evil deeds back on his own head."

Then David sent messengers to speak to Abigail about marrying him. ⁴⁰ When David's servants came to Abigail at Carmel, they said to her, "David sent us to bring you to him as a wife."

⁴¹ She stood up, paid homage with her face to the ground, and said, "Here I am, your servant, a slave to wash the feet of my lord's servants." ⁴² Then Abigail got up quickly, and with her five female servants accompanying her, rode on the donkey following David's messengers. And so she became his wife.

⁴³ David also married Ahinoam of Jezreel, and the two of them became his wives. ⁴⁴ But Saul gave his daughter Michal, David's wife, to Palti son of Laish, who was from Gallim.

Lesson 12 Questions

1. **What does the author tell us about Nabal and Abigail at the opening of the story? In what ways does Abigail exemplify wisdom? How does Nabal live up to his name?**

2. What clues in the text tell us that Nabal has plenty to spare for David and his men?

3. **Look closely at the language Abigail uses in her speech to David. Circle repeated words and highlight similar phrases. What persuasion techniques does she use? How does her unique position as a woman disrupt David's plans?**

4. Abigail's quick reaction suggests that this isn't the first time she's had to maneuver carefully to prevent disaster with Nabal. Not only does she deter David from sin, but she also preserves her entire household from David's destructive revenge.[51] How could her reaction provide a model for a godly woman's response to sinful behavior, whether it is egregious like Nabal's or more minor? In what ways does Abigail's cultural context leave her in need of divine intervention? What does a godly response to a family member's sin look like today?

5. David listens to the counsel of Abigail. What other stories does this mirror? Does this go well for David? Why or why not?

6. **God has not abandoned Abigail, even in the midst of what must have been a dark home life. In what ways does God provide for her safety? How does Abigail participate in keeping herself and her household safe? What could God's provision of safety look like in today's culture?**

7. We could view this story as a classic fairy tale—the villain has locked away a beautiful princess who is rescued by a knight in shining armor. And yes, Nabal does make a good villain, but both Abigail and David defy simple stereotypes. What have we learned about Abigail that humanizes her?

8. How is God's providence at work in this story? How have you seen God's divine care and intervention in your own life?

Lesson 12
Prayer

In this story we see a picture of Wisdom versus the Fool. Read the description of Lady Wisdom found in Proverbs 8 and 9. Consider three ways that you would like to grow in wisdom based on what you have learned in this lesson. Ask in faith for God to work in your heart, trusting the promise of James 1:5: "Now if any of you lacks wisdom, he should ask God—who gives to all generously and ungrudgingly—and it will be given to him."

Bathsheba

Character Portrait

Who	King David's eighth wife, the widow of Uriah, and the Queen Mother of Israel during Solomon's reign
When	1005–965 BC
Where	Jerusalem

Study Tool

Divine Authorship — *Following God's Agenda*

Bathsheba's story is the one that most tempts me to turn to Google. When I have questions about a particular text, I appreciate being able to glean from the wisdom of biblical scholars who have much more experience and understanding. And I *really* want to know—what exactly happened between David and Bathsheba? Was she raped? Was she vying for a social upgrade? But before we start searching online for answers to our questions, we should take a close look at the story for ourselves. An important foundation for understanding the Bible is to listen for what God is trying to say to us. The reality is, sometimes we have questions that the author is not interested in answering.[52]

If you do decide to ask the Internet, search carefully and keep in mind that algorithms prioritize popularity, not accuracy. Look for articles from established Christian publications and read the author bios. Not everyone with a seminary degree is a truthful resource, but those who have taken the time to study and submit their research for peer review may offer more useful information. Several websites and apps also offer access to Bible commentaries from theologians who have devoted their life to studying Scripture. After you have read others' reflections, go back to the text of Scripture to see how they match up.

Lesson 12
Passage

David is now king over all of Israel and lives in Jerusalem, which he established as the nation's capital. On the battlefield, God has given David great success and has affirmed his covenant with the people of Israel through David's family line. God promises to establish not just a large and fruitful family, but an eternal kingdom through David. He reminds the people of Israel that their faithfulness to God's way of living will lead to blessing. Meanwhile, at home, David begins to make some moral compromises.

2 SAMUEL 11

¹ In the spring when kings march out to war, David sent Joab with his officers and all Israel. They destroyed the Ammonites and besieged Rabbah, but David remained in Jerusalem.

² One evening David got up from his bed and strolled around on the roof of the palace. From the roof he saw a woman bathing — a very beautiful woman. ³ So David sent someone to inquire about her, and he said, "Isn't this Bathsheba, daughter of Eliam and wife of Uriah the Hethite?"

⁴ David sent messengers to get her, and when she came to him, he slept with her. Now she had just been purifying herself from her uncleanness. Afterward, she returned home. ⁵ The woman conceived and sent word to inform David, "I am pregnant."

⁶ David sent orders to Joab: "Send me Uriah the Hethite." So Joab sent Uriah to David. ⁷ When Uriah came to him, David asked how Joab and the troops were doing and how the war was going. ⁸ Then he said to Uriah, "Go down to your house and wash your feet." So Uriah left the palace, and a gift from the king followed him. ⁹ But Uriah slept at the door of the palace with all his master's servants; he did not go down to his house.

¹⁰ When it was reported to David, "Uriah didn't go home," David questioned Uriah, "Haven't you just come from a journey? Why didn't you go home?"

¹¹ Uriah answered David, "The ark, Israel, and Judah are dwelling in tents, and my master Joab and his soldiers are camping in the open field. How can I enter my house to eat and drink and sleep with my wife? As surely as you live and by your life, I will not do this!"

¹² "Stay here today also," David said to Uriah, "and tomorrow I will send you back." So Uriah stayed in Jerusalem that day and the next. ¹³ Then David invited Uriah to eat and drink with him, and David got him drunk. He went out in the evening to lie down on his cot with his master's servants, but he did not go home.

URIAH'S DEATH ARRANGED

¹⁴ The next morning David wrote a letter to Joab and sent it with Uriah. ¹⁵ In the letter he wrote:

> Put Uriah at the front of the fiercest fighting, then withdraw from him so that he is struck down and dies.

¹⁶ When Joab was besieging the city, he put Uriah in the place where he knew the best enemy soldiers were. ¹⁷ Then the men of the city came out and attacked Joab, and some of the men from David's soldiers fell in battle; Uriah the Hethite also died.

¹⁸ Joab sent someone to report to David all the details of the battle. ¹⁹ He commanded the messenger, "When you've finished telling the king all the details of the battle— ²⁰ if the king's anger gets stirred up and he asks you, 'Why did you get so close to the

city to fight? Didn't you realize they would shoot from the top of the wall? [21] At Thebez, who struck Abimelech son of Jerubbesheth? Didn't a woman drop an upper millstone on him from the top of the wall so that he died? Why did you get so close to the wall?' — then say, 'Your servant Uriah the Hethite is dead also.'" [22] Then the messenger left.

When he arrived, he reported to David all that Joab had sent him to tell. [23] The messenger reported to David, "The men gained the advantage over us and came out against us in the field, but we counterattacked right up to the entrance of the city gate. [24] However, the archers shot down on your servants from the top of the wall, and some of the king's servants died. Your servant Uriah the Hethite is also dead."

[25] David told the messenger, "Say this to Joab: 'Don't let this matter upset you because the sword devours all alike. Intensify your fight against the city and demolish it.' Encourage him."

[26] When Uriah's wife heard that her husband, Uriah, had died, she mourned for him. [27] When the time of mourning ended, David had her brought to his house. She became his wife and bore him a son. However, the LORD considered what David had done to be evil.

2 SAMUEL 12:1–25

NATHAN'S PARABLE AND DAVID'S REPENTANCE

[1] So the LORD sent Nathan to David. When he arrived, he said to him:

> There were two men in a certain city, one rich and the other poor.
> [2] The rich man had very large flocks and herds, [3] but the poor man had nothing except one small ewe lamb that he had bought. He raised her, and she grew up with him and with his children. From his meager food she would eat, from his cup she would drink, and in his arms she would sleep. She was like a daughter to him. [4] Now a traveler came to the rich man, but the rich man could not bring himself to take one of his own sheep or cattle to prepare for the traveler who had come to him. Instead, he took the poor man's lamb and prepared it for his guest.

[5] David was infuriated with the man and said to Nathan, "As the LORD lives, the man who did this deserves to die! [6] Because he has done this thing and shown no pity, he must pay four lambs for that lamb."

[7] Nathan replied to David, "You are the man! This is what the LORD God of Israel says: 'I anointed you king over Israel, and I rescued you from Saul. [8] I gave your master's house to you and your master's wives into your arms, and I gave you the house of Israel and Judah, and if that was not enough, I would have given you even more.

[9] Why then have you despised the LORD's command by doing what I consider evil? You struck down Uriah the Hethite with the sword and took his wife as your own wife — you murdered him with the Ammonite's sword. [10] Now therefore, the sword will never leave your house because you despised me and took the wife of Uriah the Hethite to be your own wife.'

What is a royal harem?

The Bible records information about historical realities that are not always intended to be guiding principles. A careful reader learns to discern the difference between *what is* versus *what should be* by looking at how God shapes his story. For example, we know that God elevates David to the throne because he is a godly man. We also see very clear examples of David's failure because he is human and imperfect like the rest of us. As we consider David's family structure, it is helpful to understand the cultural acceptance of polygamy, while keeping in mind its specific prohibition for Israel's kings[53] and the Bible's thematic preference for monogamy overall. ❸ Like other rulers in his day, David has already married a number of wives. After her husband is murdered, Bathsheba joins Abigail and at least six others in David's royal harem.

The term *harem* deserves some explanation, since it often holds an illicit connotation for us today. The historical reality is a bit more complex—*harem* is a generic word that can either refer to the private area of a house where women and their attendants lived or to the group of women themselves. The size of a man's harem corresponded to his wealth and status, and for ancient Middle Eastern royalty, adding wives to the harem was a way to cement political alliances. Inside these often-secluded women's quarters, life was organized under the leadership of either the first or favored wife or the king's mother. Eunuchs guarded the women and trained them in expectations for court life and a trade or art form that would be useful to please the king. In addition to wives and concubines, the harem might also include musicians, bathers, dancers, and poets. The wives raised their children alongside one another, but not always peaceably, competing for resources, status, and access to the king. While not quite a personal brothel, a harem was still a group of women to which the king had exclusive sexual access, and any attendant or entertainer could be elevated or used at his disposal.[54]

To understand the experience of David's wives, we must recognize that joining a royal harem would be unique in its luxuries and proximity to the king, but not surprising in its household structure. We could expect Bathsheba to struggle personally with the transition from losing her husband and first child to navigating this new community and lifestyle. At the same time, society assumed polygamy for its rulers and Bathsheba would have expected her preferences to always take a backseat to the desires of the king. The repentant David treats her with kindness, but Bathsheba will have a lot to learn as she adjusts to life among the other wives.

11 "This is what the LORD says, 'I am going to bring disaster on you from your own family: I will take your wives and give them to another before your very eyes, and he will sleep with them in broad daylight. 12 You acted in secret, but I will do this before all Israel and in broad daylight.'"

13 David responded to Nathan, "I have sinned against the LORD."

Then Nathan replied to David, "And the LORD has taken away your sin; you will not die. 14 However, because you treated the LORD with such contempt in this matter, the son born to you will die." 15 Then Nathan went home.

THE DEATH OF BATHSHEBA'S SON

The LORD struck the baby that Uriah's wife had borne to David, and he became deathly ill. 16 David pleaded with God for the boy. He fasted, went home, and spent the night lying on the ground. 17 The elders of his house stood beside him to get him up from the ground, but he was unwilling and would not eat anything with them.

18 On the seventh day the baby died. But David's servants were afraid to tell him the baby was dead. They said, "Look, while the baby was alive, we spoke to him, and he wouldn't listen to us. So how can we tell him the baby is dead? He may do something desperate."

19 When David saw that his servants were whispering to each other, he guessed that the baby was dead. So he asked his servants, "Is the baby dead?"

"He is dead," they replied.

20 Then David got up from the ground. He washed, anointed himself, changed his clothes, went to the LORD's house, and worshiped. Then he went home and requested something to eat. So they served him food, and he ate.

21 His servants asked him, "Why have you done this? While the baby was alive, you fasted and wept, but when he died, you got up and ate food."

22 He answered, "While the baby was alive, I fasted and wept because I thought, 'Who knows? The LORD may be gracious to me and let him live.' 23 But now that he is dead, why should I fast? Can I bring him back again? I'll go to him, but he will never return to me."

24 Then David comforted his wife Bathsheba; he went to her and slept with her. She gave birth to a son and named him Solomon. The LORD loved him, 25 and he sent a message through the prophet Nathan, who named him Jedidiah, because of the LORD.

We catch up with Bathsheba a few decades later, as David is dying.

1 KINGS 1:11-31

NATHAN'S AND BATHSHEBA'S APPEALS

11 Then Nathan said to Bathsheba, Solomon's mother, "Have you not heard that Adonijah son of Haggith has become king and our Lord David does not know it? 12 Now please come and let me advise you. Save your life and the life of your son Solomon. 13 Go, approach King David and say to him, 'My lord the king, did you not swear to your servant: Your son Solomon is to become king after me, and he is the one who is to sit on my throne? So why has Adonijah become king?' 14 At that moment, while you are still there speaking with the king, I'll come in after you and confirm your words."

15 So Bathsheba went to the king in his bedroom. Since the king was very old, Abishag the Shunammite was attending to him. 16 Bathsheba knelt low and paid homage to the king, and he asked, "What do you want?"

17 She replied, "My lord, you swore to your servant by the LORD your God, 'Your son Solomon is to become king after me, and he is the one who is to sit on my throne.' 18 Now look, Adonijah has become king. And, my lord the king, you didn't know it. 19 He has lavishly sacrificed oxen, fattened cattle, and sheep. He invited all the king's sons, the priest Abiathar, and Joab the commander of the army, but he did not invite your servant Solomon. 20 Now, my lord the king, the eyes of all Israel are on you to tell them who will sit on the throne of my lord the king after him. 21 Otherwise, when my lord the king rests with his ancestors, I and my son Solomon will be regarded as criminals."

22 At that moment, while she was still speaking with the king, the prophet Nathan arrived, 23 and it was announced to the king, "The prophet Nathan is here." He came into the king's presence and paid homage to him with his face to the ground.

24 "My lord the king," Nathan said, "did you say, 'Adonijah is to become king after me, and he is the one who is to sit on my throne'? 25 For today he went down and lavishly sacrificed oxen, fattened cattle, and sheep. He invited all the sons of the king, the commanders of the army, and the priest Abiathar. And look!

They're eating and drinking in his presence, and they're saying, 'Long live King Adonijah! ' 26 But he did not invite me — me, your servant — or the priest Zadok or Benaiah son of Jehoiada or your servant Solomon. 27 I'm certain my lord the king would not have let this happen without letting your servant know who will sit on my lord the king's throne after him."

SOLOMON CONFIRMED KING

28 King David responded by saying, "Call in Bathsheba for me." So she came into the king's presence and stood before him. 29 The king swore an oath and said, "As the LORD lives, who has redeemed my life from every difficulty, 30 just as I swore to you by the LORD God of Israel: Your son Solomon is to become king after me, and he is the one who is to sit on my throne in my place, that is exactly what I will do this very day."

31 Bathsheba knelt low with her face to the ground, paying homage to the king, and said, "May my lord King David live forever!"

Family Tree

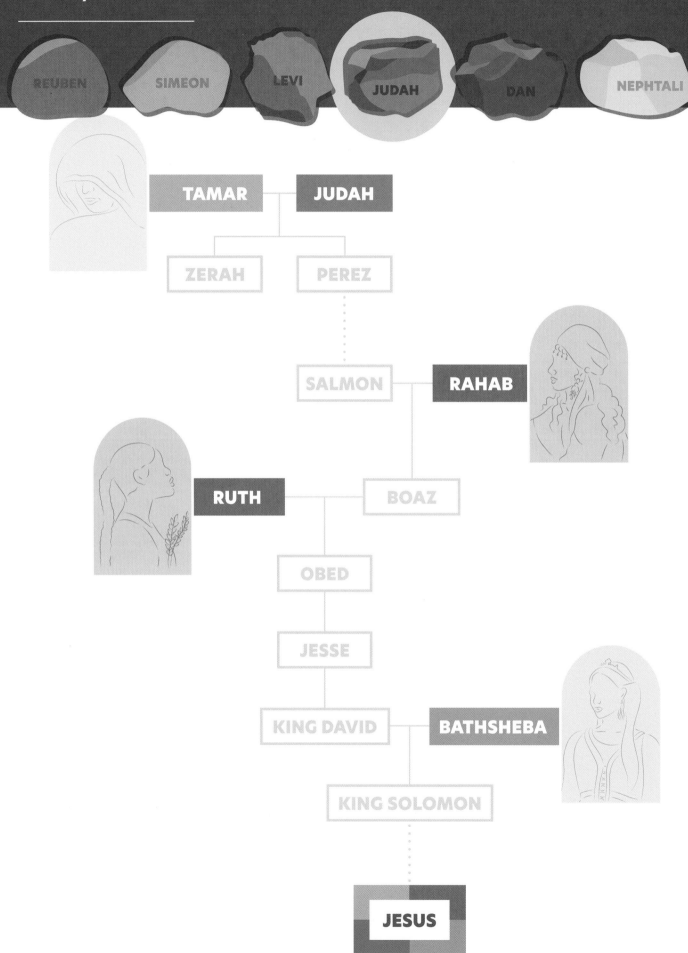

REUBEN SIMEON LEVI JUDAH DAN NEPHTALI

TAMAR — JUDAH

ZERAH PEREZ

SALMON — RAHAB

RUTH BOAZ

OBED

JESSE

KING DAVID — BATHSHEBA

KING SOLOMON

JESUS

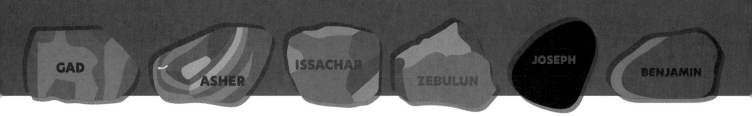

Remember what we learned about the women in the Exodus story and their role as partners in keeping the oral tradition of scripture alive? Each of the women we've studied thus far participated in sharing the great work God had done in her own story. They would have told these stories to their young sons, shaping their moral values and helping them remember the traditions of their fathers. ❻

Sarah
Mother of Isaac

Leah
Mother to Judah

Miriam
Sister to Moses

Rahab
Mother of Boaz[55]

Naomi and Ruth
Grandmother and mother to Obed, respectively

Deborah
Mother of Israel, advisor to Barak

Hannah
Mother of the prophet Samuel

Bathsheba
Mother to King Solomon

Lesson 13 Questions

1. Bathing wasn't a daily ritual for ancient cultures the way that it is today. The author makes a point to tell us that Bathsheba was "purifying herself from her uncleanness," which is a reference to the ritual purification required after menstruation. What do these details tell us about Bathsheba's family situation and her religious practice?

2. Nathan crafts a piercing parable rather than directly confronting David for taking another man's wife. Who parallels Bathsheba in Nathan's story? Whom does Nathan hold accountable? How does Nathan's interaction with David help us better understand Bathsheba?

3. David desires Bathsheba and does what seems wise in his own eyes. He takes her, and then, when he realizes the consequences of his action, he tries covering himself by killing Uriah. Is he able to hide his sin from the Lord? How does this story impact your understanding of sin, repentance, and the suffering that results from being sinned against?

4. The group of David's wives and children was relatively small, especially compared to other royal harems in this period, so the women may have developed close relationships over the years. Imagine how Abigail might have influenced Bathsheba. In what ways might the two women have been able to relate to one another?

5. We jumped ahead in our reading to the end of David's life and this time find Nathan and Bathsheba working together. What goal do they accomplish? How does David treat Bathsheba during this interaction? What does this part of the story tell us about her reputation with Nathan and David?

6. **The books of Proverbs, Ecclesiastes, and Song of Songs are attributed to Bathsheba's son, King Solomon, who was called the wisest of all kings.[56] Who were his primary influences during his childhood? In what ways does his success honor Bathsheba?**

7. Consider the four women listed in Matthew 1 of Jesus' genealogy—Rahab, Tamar, Ruth, and Bathsheba. If you were highlighting the important women in the line of the Messiah, are they the ones you would pick? What does this show you about who belongs in God's family? How might this insight impact the way you view women in your church community?

8. David is repentant for his sin against Bathsheba and Uriah. God forgives his sin, but the consequences of his actions cannot be undone. How does God protect and care for Bathsheba? Does she experience restoration and repair? How does her story offer hope for victims?

Lesson 13
Prayer

Biblical womanhood looks like teaching and nurturing the next generation, whether they are your biological children or those in the family of God that you mentor and influence. Look back at your list from Lesson 8. Pray that those three people would grow in wisdom and understanding of the Lord like Solomon. Ask God to provide a specific opportunity for you to invest spiritually in one of them this week.

LESSON 14
Vashti & Esther

Character Portrait

Vashti	The first queen of Ahasuerus
Esther	A young Jewish woman who becomes the next queen and saves her people
When	485–465 BC
Where	The Persian city of Susa

Study Tool
Divine Authorship — *Historical Accuracy*

While the Bible often references historical events, we must remember that the overarching goal is to tell God's story, not give a comprehensive understanding of the political or social structures of the time.[57] While some have suggested that the book of Esther should be read as a parable or allegory, the text itself assumes a historical context,[58] so we will treat it as such, paying attention to God's agenda in the story rather than questions of chronology. As you read this narrative, notice which details are included and how those shape our understanding of God's character and interaction with his people. •

Lesson 14
Passage

After King Solomon's reign, the Israelite monarchy devolved into cycle after cycle of turning from God and falling into the hands of other nations. First the kingdom broke into two factions, splitting Judah and Benjamin from the other ten tribes. Then, all of the tribes were exiled into various surrounding nations. We meet Esther and her cousin Mordecai in the capital of Persia.

Esther's Ancestry

The tribe of Benjamin was one of the two tribes who were eventually allowed to return to the Promised Land after the Babylonian exile in 586 BC.[59] Esther's relationship to Benjamin means she is also a descendent of Rachel.

ESTHER 1

¹ These events took place during the days of Ahasuerus, who ruled 127 provinces from India to Cush.

² In those days King Ahasuerus reigned from his royal throne in the fortress at Susa. ³ He held a feast in the third year of his reign for all his officials and staff, the army of Persia and Media, the nobles, and the officials from the provinces. ⁴ He displayed the glorious wealth of his kingdom and the magnificent splendor of his greatness for a total of 180 days.

⁵ At the end of this time, the king held a week-long banquet in the garden courtyard of the royal palace for all the people, from the greatest to the least, who were present in the fortress of Susa. ⁶ White and blue linen hangings were fastened with fine white and purple linen cords to silver rods on marble columns. Gold and silver couches were arranged on a mosaic pavement of red feldspar, marble, mother-of-pearl, and precious stones.

⁷ Drinks were served in an array of gold goblets, each with a different design. Royal wine flowed freely, according to the king's bounty. ⁸ The drinking was according to royal decree: "There are no restrictions." The king had ordered every wine steward in his household to serve whatever each person wanted. ⁹ Queen Vashti also gave a feast for the women of King Ahasuerus's palace.

¹⁰ On the seventh day, when the king was feeling good from the wine, Ahasuerus commanded Mehuman, Biztha, Harbona, Bigtha, Abagtha, Zethar, and Carkas — the seven eunuchs who personally served him — ¹¹ to bring Queen Vashti before him with her royal crown. He wanted to show off her beauty to the people and the officials, because she was very beautiful. ¹² But Queen Vashti refused to come at the king's command that was delivered by his eunuchs. The king became furious and his anger burned within him.

THE KING'S DECREE

¹³ The king consulted the wise men who understood the times, for it was his normal procedure to confer with experts in law and justice. ¹⁴ The most trusted ones were Carshena, Shethar, Admatha, Tarshish, Meres, Marsena, and Memucan. They were the seven officials of Persia and Media who had personal access to the king and occupied the highest positions in the kingdom. ¹⁵ The king asked, "According to the law, what should be done with Queen Vashti, since she refused to obey King Ahasuerus's command that was delivered by the eunuchs?"

¹⁶ Memucan said in the presence of the king and his officials, "Queen Vashti has wronged not only the king, but all the officials and the peoples who are in every one of King Ahasuerus's provinces. ¹⁷ For the queen's action will become public knowledge to all the women and cause them to despise their husbands and say, 'King Ahasuerus ordered Queen Vashti brought before him, but she did not come.' ¹⁸ Before this day is over, the noble women of Persia and Media who hear about the queen's act will say the same thing to all the king's officials, resulting in more contempt and fury.

¹⁹ "If it meets the king's approval, he should personally issue a royal decree. Let it be recorded in the laws of the Persians and Medes, so that it cannot be revoked: Vashti

is not to enter King Ahasuerus's presence, and her royal position is to be given to another woman who is more worthy than she. ²⁰ The decree the king issues will be heard throughout his vast kingdom, so all women will honor their husbands, from the greatest to the least."

²¹ The king and his counselors approved the proposal, and he followed Memucan's advice. ²² He sent letters to all the royal provinces, to each province in its own script and to each ethnic group in its own language, that every man should be master of his own house and speak in the language of his own people.

ESTHER 2

THE SEARCH FOR A NEW QUEEN

¹ Some time later, when King Ahasuerus's rage had cooled down, he remembered Vashti, what she had done, and what was decided against her.

² The king's personal attendants suggested, "Let a search be made for beautiful young virgins for the king. ³ Let the king appoint commissioners in each province of his kingdom, so that they may gather all the beautiful young virgins to the harem at the fortress of Susa. Put them under the supervision of Hegai, the king's eunuch, keeper of the women, and give them the required beauty treatments. ⁴ Then the young woman who pleases the king will become queen instead of Vashti." This suggestion pleased the king, and he did accordingly.

⁵ In the fortress of Susa, there was a Jewish man named Mordecai son of Jair, son of Shimei, son of Kish, a Benjaminite. ⁶ Kish had been taken into exile from Jerusalem with the other captives when King Nebuchadnezzar of Babylon took King Jeconiah of Judah into exile. ⁷ Mordecai was the legal guardian of his cousin Hadassah (that is, Esther), because she had no father or mother. The young woman had a beautiful figure and was extremely good-looking. When her father and mother died, Mordecai had adopted her as his own daughter.

⁸ When the king's command and edict became public knowledge and when many young women were gathered at the fortress of Susa under Hegai's supervision, Esther was taken to the palace, into the supervision of Hegai, keeper of the women. ⁹ The young woman pleased him and gained his favor so that he accelerated the process of the beauty treatments and the special diet that she received. He assigned seven hand-picked female servants to her from the palace and transferred her and her servants to the harem's best quarters.

¹⁰ Esther did not reveal her ethnicity or her family background, because Mordecai had ordered her not to make them known.

¹¹ Every day Mordecai took a walk in front of the harem's courtyard to learn how Esther was doing and to see what was happening to her.

¹² During the year before each young woman's turn to go to King Ahasuerus, the harem regulation required her to receive beauty treatments with oil of myrrh for six months and then with perfumes and cosmetics for another six months. ¹³ When the young woman would go to the king, she was given whatever she requested to take with her from the harem to the palace. ¹⁴ She would go in the evening, and in the morning she would return to a second harem under the supervision of the king's eunuch Shaashgaz, keeper of the concubines. She never went to the king again, unless he desired her and summoned her by name.

ESTHER BECOMES QUEEN

¹⁵ Esther was the daughter of Abihail, the uncle of Mordecai who had adopted her as his own daughter. When her turn came to go to the king, she did not ask for anything except what Hegai, the king's eunuch, keeper of the women, suggested. Esther gained favor in the eyes of everyone who saw her.

¹⁶ She was taken to King Ahasuerus in the palace in the tenth month, the month Tebeth, in the seventh year of his reign. ¹⁷ The king loved Esther more than all the other women. She won more favor and approval from him than did any of the other virgins. He placed the royal crown on her head and made her queen in place of Vashti. ¹⁸ The king held a great banquet for all his officials and staff. It was Esther's banquet. He freed his provinces from tax payments and gave gifts worthy of the king's bounty.

MORDECAI SAVES THE KING

¹⁹ When the virgins were gathered a second time, Mordecai was sitting at the King's Gate. ²⁰ Esther still did not reveal her family background or her ethnicity, as Mordecai had directed. She obeyed Mordecai's orders, as she always had while he raised her.

²¹ During those days while Mordecai was sitting at the King's Gate, Bigthan and Teresh, two of the king's eunuchs who guarded the entrance, became infuriated and planned to assassinate King Ahasuerus. ²² When Mordecai learned of the plot, he reported it to Queen Esther, and she told the king on Mordecai's behalf. ²³ When the report was investigated and verified, both men were hanged on the gallows. This event was recorded in the Historical Record in the king's presence.

Lesson 14 Questions

1. **List five traits you observe about Ahasuerus's character from his interactions with Vashti and with his friends. What do we learn about this king and his kingdom in the opening scenes? How does this contrast with the type of kingdom God wants to build?**

Ahasuerus's Kingdom Priorities	God's Kingdom Priorities

2. What is Vashti expected to do? How is she treated when she defies those expectations? Based on her story, how might we expect Esther to be treated?

3. The book of Esther sets up two partnerships as foils of each other. In this lesson, we will look at the first pair. What does the partnership between King Ahasuerus and Vashti look like? Considering her role as the head of his harem and the details we learn about their interaction, do you find their marriage admirable? Why or why not?

4. **Not only is Ahasuerus personally offended by Vashti's action, but his friends are worried that her behavior will inspire other women to disobey their husbands. How is Ahasuerus's idea of a good wife different from what the Bible teaches? In what ways does their pagan culture inform these expectations? Is your idea of a good marriage influenced more by your own culture or by the Bible?**

5. The harem that Ahasuerus is building is very different from what we looked at with David's wives. He has systematically collected all the young women from surrounding villages and plans to audition each one to determine her rank and purpose in his household. How would removing all eligible women from the surrounding communities impact those communities? How would this social obligation affect Esther and the other young women? Consider the various reactions that girls might have had to the king's edict.

6. **Sometimes the Bible gives us explicit value judgments for a particular character (like we saw with Nabal and Abigail), but more often than not, the writer allows a person's actions to reveal their heart. What details does the author give us about Esther? Underline actions done to or for her and circle actions she takes for herself. What is your impression of Esther thus far? What job skills or qualifications does she have for leadership?**

7. Whether she likes it or not, Esther is drafted into an unusual new community that requires a particularly strange form of education. How do the eunuchs, the other women, and eventually the king respond to her? What do their reactions show us about the traits they value in a woman? Do any of their values align with God's values?

8. Vashti, Esther, and Mordecai's lives have been upended, and we haven't seen any mention of God in this story. Has he forgotten them? What do you do when God seems absent in your own life?

Lesson 14
Prayer

Esther grew up in a religious home within a completely pagan culture. Her family are not only exiles from their homeland of Israel, but she is now further exiled from them into a secluded harem. Who are the Esthers in your life? Pray for those who may feel like outcasts in your community and ask God how you might uniquely love them this week.

Esther, Part 2

Character Portrait

Who	A young Jewish woman who becomes the next queen and saves her people
When	485–465 BC
Where	The Persian city of Susa

Study Tool
Story Arrangement — *Where is God?*

Esther is the only book in the Bible where God is not mentioned by name—but this is no mistake. During these difficult years, when the people of Israel lived as exiles among pagan nations, it was easy to feel like God had forgotten them. Omitting a direct reference to God builds tension in the story as we ask: Who could be behind all these unbelievable coincidences? Who would use the person with the weakest social capital to shame the strong and powerful? The original readers would view these twists and turns as God's intervention, rather than chance or fate.[60] Esther's story does not offer life advice for how to handle morally ambiguous situations. Instead, it reveals how God moves in spite of them. Yes, we can admire brave and faithful choices that Esther makes, but God is the true hero, working behind the scenes to orchestrate salvation for his people once again. •

Lesson 15
Passage

Now that Esther has become queen, the narrative shifts focus to other palace intrigue. Ahasuerus has promoted Haman as his highest official and commands everyone to bow down to Haman. Mordecai refuses to worship him, so Haman plots revenge by convincing Ahasuerus to kill everyone throughout Persia who is of Jewish ethnicity.

ESTHER 4
MORDECAI APPEALS TO ESTHER

[1] When Mordecai learned all that had occurred, he tore his clothes, put on sackcloth and ashes, went into the middle of the city, and cried loudly and bitterly. [2] He went only as far as the King's Gate, since the law prohibited anyone wearing sackcloth from entering the King's Gate. [3] There was great mourning among the Jewish people in every province where the king's command and edict reached. They fasted, wept, and lamented, and many lay in sackcloth and ashes.

[4] Esther's female servants and her eunuchs came and reported the news to her, and the queen was overcome with fear. She sent clothes for Mordecai to wear so that he would take off his sackcloth, but he did not accept them. [5] Esther summoned Hathach, one of the king's eunuchs who attended her, and dispatched him to Mordecai to learn what he was doing and why. [6] So Hathach went out to Mordecai in the city square in front of the King's Gate. [7] Mordecai told him everything that had happened as well as the exact amount of money Haman had promised to pay the royal treasury for the slaughter of the Jews.

[8] Mordecai also gave him a copy of the written decree issued in Susa ordering their destruction, so that Hathach might show it to Esther, explain it to her, and command her to approach the king, implore his favor, and plead with him personally for her people. [9] Hathach came and repeated Mordecai's response to Esther.

[10] Esther spoke to Hathach and commanded him to tell Mordecai, [11] "All the royal officials and the people of the royal provinces know that one law applies to every man or woman who approaches the king in the inner courtyard and who has not been summoned — the death penalty — unless the king extends the gold scepter, allowing that person to live. I have not been summoned to appear before the king for the last thirty days." [12] Esther's response was reported to Mordecai.

[13] Mordecai told the messenger to reply to Esther, "Don't think that you will escape the fate of all the Jews because you are in the king's palace. [14] If you keep silent at this time, relief and deliverance will come to the Jewish people from another place, but you and your father's family will be destroyed. Who knows, perhaps you have come to your royal position for such a time as this."

[15] Esther sent this reply to Mordecai: [16] "Go and assemble all the Jews who can be found in Susa and fast for me. Don't eat or drink for three days, night or day. I and my female servants will also fast in the same way. After that, I will go to the king even if it is against the law. If I perish, I perish." [17] So Mordecai went and did everything Esther had commanded him.

ESTHER 5
ESTHER APPROACHES THE KING

[1] On the third day, Esther dressed in her royal clothing and stood in the inner courtyard of the palace facing it. The king was sitting on his royal throne in the royal courtroom, facing its entrance. [2] As soon as the king saw Queen Esther standing in the courtyard, she gained favor with him. The king extended the gold scepter in his hand toward Esther, and she approached and touched the tip of the scepter.

³ "What is it, Queen Esther?" the king asked her. "Whatever you want, even to half the kingdom, will be given to you."

⁴ "If it pleases the king," Esther replied, "may the king and Haman come today to the banquet I have prepared for them."

⁵ The king said, "Hurry, and get Haman so we can do as Esther has requested." So the king and Haman went to the banquet Esther had prepared.

⁶ While drinking the wine, the king asked Esther, "Whatever you ask will be given to you. Whatever you want, even to half the kingdom, will be done."

⁷ Esther answered, "This is my petition and my request: ⁸ If I have found favor in the eyes of the king, and if it pleases the king to grant my petition and perform my request, may the king and Haman come to the banquet I will prepare for them. Tomorrow I will do what the king has asked."

⁹ That day Haman left full of joy and in good spirits. But when Haman saw Mordecai at the King's Gate, and Mordecai didn't rise or tremble in fear at his presence, Haman was filled with rage toward Mordecai. ¹⁰ Yet Haman controlled himself and went home. He sent for his friends and his wife Zeresh to join him. ¹¹ Then Haman described for them his glorious wealth and his many sons. He told them all how the king had honored him and promoted him in rank over the other officials and the royal staff. ¹² "What's more," Haman added, "Queen Esther invited no one but me to join the king at the banquet she had prepared. I am invited again tomorrow to join her with the king. ¹³ Still, none of this satisfies me since I see Mordecai the Jew sitting at the King's Gate all the time."

¹⁴ His wife Zeresh and all his friends told him, "Have them build a gallows seventy-five feet tall. Ask the king in the morning to hang Mordecai on it. Then go to the banquet with the king and enjoy yourself." The advice pleased Haman, so he had the gallows constructed.

ESTHER 6

MORDECAI HONORED BY THE KING

¹ That night sleep escaped the king, so he ordered the book recording daily events to be brought and read to the king. ² They found the written report of how Mordecai had informed on Bigthana and Teresh, two of the king's eunuchs who guarded the entrance, when they planned to assassinate King Ahasuerus. ³ The king inquired, "What honor and special recognition have been given to Mordecai for this act?"

The king's personal attendants replied, "Nothing has been done for him."

⁴ The king asked, "Who is in the court?" Now Haman was just entering the outer court of the palace to ask the king to hang Mordecai on the gallows he had prepared for him.

⁵ The king's attendants answered him, "Haman is there, standing in the court."

"Have him enter," the king ordered. 6 Haman entered, and the king asked him, "What should be done for the man the king wants to honor?"

Haman thought to himself, "Who is it the king would want to honor more than me?" 7 Haman told the king, "For the man the king wants to honor: 8 Have them bring a royal garment that the king himself has worn and a horse the king himself has ridden, which has a royal crown on its head. 9 Put the garment and the horse under the charge of one of the king's most noble officials. Have them clothe the man the king wants to honor, parade him on the horse through the city square, and call out before him, 'This is what is done for the man the king wants to honor.'"

10 The king told Haman, "Hurry, and do just as you proposed. Take a garment and a horse for Mordecai the Jew, who is sitting at the King's Gate. Do not leave out anything you have suggested."

11 So Haman took the garment and the horse. He clothed Mordecai and paraded him through the city square, calling out before him, "This is what is done for the man the king wants to honor."

12 Then Mordecai returned to the King's Gate, but Haman hurried off for home, mournful and with his head covered. 13 Haman told his wife Zeresh and all his friends everything that had happened. His advisers and his wife Zeresh said to him, "Since Mordecai is Jewish, and you have begun to fall before him, you won't overcome him, because your downfall is certain." 14 While they were still speaking with him, the king's eunuchs arrived and rushed Haman to the banquet Esther had prepared.

ESTHER 7
HAMAN IS EXECUTED

1 The king and Haman came to feast with Esther the queen. 2 Once again, on the second day while drinking wine, the king asked Esther, "Queen Esther, whatever you ask will be given to you. Whatever you seek, even to half the kingdom, will be done."

3 Queen Esther answered, "If I have found favor with you, Your Majesty, and if the king is pleased, spare my life; this is my request. And spare my people; this is my desire. 4 For my people and I have been sold to destruction, death, and annihilation. If we had merely been sold as male and female slaves, I would have kept silent. Indeed, the trouble wouldn't be worth burdening the king."

5 King Ahasuerus spoke up and asked Queen Esther, "Who is this, and where is the one who would devise such a scheme?"
6 Esther answered, "The adversary and enemy is this evil Haman."

Haman stood terrified before the king and queen. 7 The king arose in anger and went from where they were drinking wine to the palace garden. Haman remained to beg Queen Esther for his life because he realized the king was planning something terrible for him. 8 Just as the king returned from the palace garden to the banquet hall, Haman was falling on the couch where Esther was reclining. The king exclaimed, "Would he actually violate the queen while I am in the house?" As soon as the statement left the king's mouth, they covered Haman's face.

⁹ Harbona, one of the king's eunuchs, said, "There is a gallows seventy-five feet tall at Haman's house that he made for Mordecai, who gave the report that saved the king."

The king said, "Hang him on it."

¹⁰ They hanged Haman on the gallows he had prepared for Mordecai. Then the king's anger subsided.

ESTHER 8
ESTHER INTERVENES FOR THE JEWS

¹ That same day King Ahasuerus awarded Queen Esther the estate of Haman, the enemy of the Jews. Mordecai entered the king's presence because Esther had revealed her relationship to Mordecai. ² The king removed his signet ring he had recovered from Haman and gave it to Mordecai, and Esther put him in charge of Haman's estate.

³ Then Esther addressed the king again. She fell at his feet, wept, and begged him to revoke the evil of Haman the Agagite and his plot he had devised against the Jews. ⁴ The king extended the gold scepter toward Esther, so she got up and stood before the king.

⁵ She said, "If it pleases the king and I have found favor with him, if the matter seems right to the king and I am pleasing in his eyes, let a royal edict be written. Let it revoke the documents the scheming Haman son of Hammedatha the Agagite wrote to destroy the Jews who are in all the king's provinces. ⁶ For how could I bear to see the disaster that would come on my people? How could I bear to see the destruction of my relatives?"

⁷ King Ahasuerus said to Esther the queen and to Mordecai the Jew, "Look, I have given Haman's estate to Esther, and he was hanged on the gallows because he attacked the Jews. ⁸ Write in the king's name whatever pleases you concerning the Jews, and seal it with the royal signet ring. A document written in the king's name and sealed with the royal signet ring cannot be revoked."

⁹ On the twenty-third day of the third month — that is, the month Sivan — the royal scribes were summoned. Everything was written exactly as Mordecai commanded for the Jews, to the satraps, the governors, and the officials of the 127 provinces from India to Cush. The edict was written for each province in its own script, for each ethnic group in its own language, and to the Jews in their own script and language.

¹⁰ Mordecai wrote in King Ahasuerus's name and sealed the edicts with the royal signet ring. He sent the documents by mounted couriers, who rode fast horses bred in the royal stables.

¹¹ The king's edict gave the Jews in each and every city the right to assemble and defend themselves, to destroy, kill, and annihilate every ethnic and provincial army hostile to them, including women and children, and to take their possessions as spoils of war. ¹² This would take place on a single day throughout all the provinces of King Ahasuerus, on the thirteenth day of the twelfth month, the month Adar.

¹³ A copy of the text, issued as law throughout every province, was distributed to all the peoples so the Jews could be ready to avenge themselves against their enemies on that day. ¹⁴ The couriers rode out in haste on their royal horses at the king's urgent command. The law was also issued in the fortress of Susa.

¹⁵ Mordecai went from the king's presence clothed in royal blue and white, with a great gold crown and a purple robe of fine linen. The city of Susa shouted and rejoiced, ¹⁶ and the Jews celebrated with gladness, joy, and honor. ¹⁷ In every province and every city where the king's command and edict reached, gladness and joy took place among the Jews. There was a celebration and a holiday. And many of the ethnic groups of the land professed themselves to be Jews because fear of the Jews had overcome them.

Lesson 15 Questions

1. Esther gets a lot more dialogue in this part of the story. Consider your assessment of her character from Question 6 in the previous lesson. How do Esther's words and actions shift in the chapters we read today? In what ways has she grown?

2. **Ahasuerus is surrounded by "yes men"—a bunch of supporters who tell him what he wants to hear. How does Mordecai and Esther's dynamic differ? What does she do with the hard truth he shares?**

3. We've seen throughout this story that Ahasuerus is reactionary and emotional, easily swayed by those who flatter him. List the ways that Esther shrewdly uses this knowledge about him to her advantage.

4. In the last lesson, we considered the partnership between Ahasuerus and Vashti. By contrast, how do Mordecai and Esther work together? What do they each ask the other to do? Is their partnership successful? Why or why not?

5. What position do you have "for such a time as this"? How could God use your unique access, position, or ability to bless others?

6. In the covenant God made with Israel, he promises blessing when his people are faithful to him. In what ways does Esther follow God's law? In what ways does she fail? What does this story show us about God's commitment to rescue his people?

7. Esther seeks wise counsel, learning from the eunuchs and following the advice of her uncle, which shapes her ability to be successful when the people need her most. Who in your life plays a counseling role like Mordecai? What would it look like to seek and to apply the wisdom of faithful believers in this season of your life?

8. Esther may have begun as just another pretty face in the harem, but her bravery and faithful choices saved countless lives. What does her story tell us about who God raises up? What does he consider "leadership potential"?

Lesson 15
Prayer

Esther's story reminds us that
God does not forsake his people.
Write a prayer of thanksgiving
for five (or more!) ways that
God has been working behind
the scenes through seeming
coincidences in your life or in
the lives of those around you.

Thematic Recap

The women of Part Three held great influence during the Israelite kingdom and dispersion. They certainly were not perfect, and yet God invited them into his story anyway. As you read through this section, which character traits about God did you see in a new way? What messages about womanhood or yourself resonated most?

About God	*About Womanhood*	*About Myself*
Knows the depth of our pain	Using power for the good of others	
Works within families	Seeking wisdom from God, not the culture	
Hears us	Generosity and hospitality	
Intervenes in providential ways	Nurturing the next generation	
Cares about women's safety	Sinners and sufferers	

Interlude: *Heroines, Sinners, and Sufferers*

So far, we have read the stories of quite a variety of women. We considered their cultural context and their place in the larger narrative of God's story. In our study questions, we connected to their challenges, struggles, and victories as real humans, often finding insight from their stories that shapes our understanding of womanhood and points to God's expectation-shattering love.

As we meditate on the stories of women in the Bible, I hope you will continue to resist the temptation to turn each narrative into a neat and tidy morality play. It might feel simpler to cast our characters as heroes or villains (or in some cases, irrelevant background chorus) or—to use a line from Glinda in the *Wizard of Oz*—to ask them, "Are you a good witch or a bad witch?"[61] But trying to fit their stories into the boxes of saint or seductress cheapens our experience of the Bible.

Perhaps you know better than to view people as completely good or evil, but another way we sometimes err is by focusing all our attention on which choices were sinful and which were commendable. We question the morality of each action, looking to connect every negative outcome with the sin that caused it. We might have avoided creating archetypes only to lose sight of the bigger picture by sin-hunting. Instead of seeing God's intervention, God's plan, God's work on every page, we are satisfied with conclusions that put us in control. *If I can just determine the precise boundaries of sin, then maybe I can strongarm my way into the kingdom.* We end up with simplified applications like "be careful who you marry" or "never lie about your identity" that hinge our wellbeing on our ability to not sin. Or, we might assume that a given story is only relevant on the off chance we are drafted into a royal harem.

But this isn't the story the Bible is telling. God is writing his own story. Sometimes it includes clear villains and sometimes it shows us how to behave, but it is always more than that. God is working out a master plan for salvation, and he partners with humanity in the work he is doing. He invites us—women just as much as the men—to be fruitful on this earth, propagating the good news of our Creator who is Savior and Father and Friend.

Yes, the Bible has plenty to say about sin. All thoughts and actions that violate God's law condemn us to eternal separation from our good Creator. We need a redeemer and deliverer from our sin. But personal sin is only half of the problem of the Fall. Adam and Eve's choice to sin comes with a curse. The world is now full of suffering, full of brokenness, fully lacking. God's good creation was just as damaged as his relationship with humanity, so alongside the natural consequences of our own sin, we suffer in a number of ways. Other people sin against us. Societies are structured to favor those in power at the expense of outsiders. The ground itself fights our efforts to cultivate it, and nature violently attacks instead of living with us in harmony.

Biblical women are just like us. We are all sinners *and* sufferers. We see in their stories both the harm done against them and the consequences of their unwise, selfish choices. So although we resist glorifying women in the Bible as we work to contextualize their stories, we also see their full humanity. We don't use context to explain away their sin, and at the same time, we can still admire their great faith and how they whisper of our Savior to come. We might even still call them heroines, recognizing their rightful place as those who answered God's calling to participate in his work of making creation flourish. •

PART FOUR

The Disciples of Jesus

God is about to do
something **big***.*

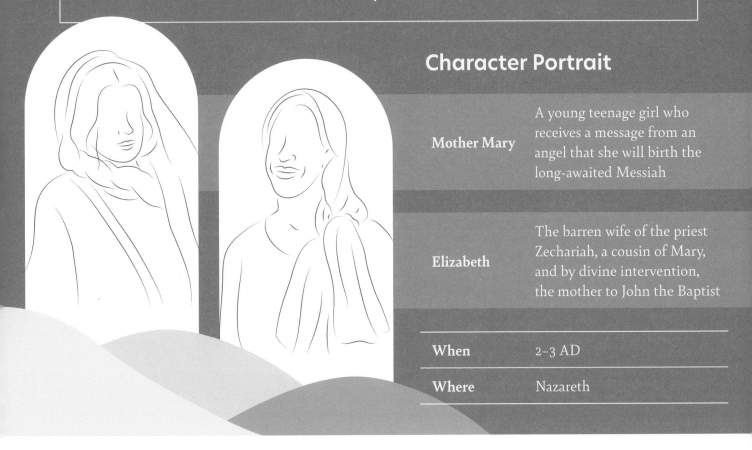

Mother Mary & Elizabeth

Character Portrait

Mother Mary	A young teenage girl who receives a message from an angel that she will birth the long-awaited Messiah
Elizabeth	The barren wife of the priest Zechariah, a cousin of Mary, and by divine intervention, the mother to John the Baptist
When	2–3 AD
Where	Nazareth

Study Tool

Meditation — *Seeing with New Eyes*

God is about to do something big. We have been listening to whispers of his plan to rescue humanity and restore Eden throughout the Old Testament. And now, he announces the grand entrance of Jesus to two very unlikely ladies. One very young and one quite old, these women were not famous or powerful. They are at opposite ends of the childbearing spectrum, united by miraculous pregnancies and even more miraculous revelations about *Emmanuel*, God with Us.

Try to read Mary's story through the eyes of a young, betrothed teen. Try on Elizabeth's perspective, too. Consider how the story unfolds if you only know the details that they know. •

Lesson 16
Passage

Many generations have passed since the Israelite people last heard from the Lord. During this 400-year silence, Jews living in exile have assimilated to their new cultures and those who returned to the Promised Land continue to wait for a new king to restore and deliver their people. Meanwhile, in a small country village, a young teenage girl is preparing for her wedding.

LUKE 1:26-56

26 In the sixth month, the angel Gabriel was sent by God to a town in Galilee called Nazareth, 27 to a virgin engaged to a man named Joseph, of the house of David. The virgin's name was Mary. 28 And the angel came to her and said, "Greetings, favored woman! The Lord is with you." 29 But she was deeply troubled by this statement, wondering what kind of greeting this could be. 30 Then the angel told her, "Do not be afraid, Mary, for you have found favor with God. 31 Now listen: You will conceive and give birth to a son, and you will name him Jesus. 32 He will be great and will be called the Son of the Most High, and the Lord God will give him the throne of his father David. 33 He will reign over the house of Jacob forever, and his kingdom will have no end."

34 Mary asked the angel, "How can this be, since I have not had sexual relations with a man?"

35 The angel replied to her, "The Holy Spirit will come upon you, and the power of the Most High will overshadow you. Therefore, the holy one to be born will be called the Son of God. 36 And consider your relative Elizabeth — even she has conceived a son in her old age, and this is the sixth month for her who was called childless. 37 For nothing will be impossible with God."

38 "See, I am the Lord's servant," said Mary. "May it happen to me as you have said." Then the angel left her.

MARY'S VISIT TO ELIZABETH

39 In those days Mary set out and hurried to a town in the hill country of Judah 40 where she entered Zechariah's house and greeted Elizabeth. 41 When Elizabeth heard Mary's greeting, the baby leaped inside her, and Elizabeth was filled with the Holy Spirit. 42 Then she exclaimed with a loud cry, "Blessed are you among women, and your child will be blessed! 43 How could this happen to me, that the mother of my Lord should come to me? 44 For you see, when the sound of your greeting reached my ears, the baby leaped for joy inside me. 45 Blessed is she who has believed that the Lord would fulfill what he has spoken to her!"

MARY'S PRAISE

46 And Mary said:

> My soul magnifies the Lord,
> 47 and my spirit rejoices in God my Savior,
> 48 because he has looked with favor
> on the humble condition of his servant.
> Surely, from now on all generations
> will call me blessed,
> 49 because the Mighty One
> has done great things for me,
> and his name is holy.
> 50 His mercy is from generation to generation
> on those who fear him.

The **Upper Room** could be used as a workspace and was the most cool, comfortable place to sleep.

Storage

Food Preparation Area

The **Courtyard** was a family living space by day and a place to protect animals at night.

A **Manger** to feed the animals.

A Home in Bethlehem

Mary traveled with Joseph to his hometown of Bethlehem to be registered in a national census. The expectations of hospitality, not to mention Joseph's membership in King David's family line, would mean that he was welcome in any home in Bethlehem,[62] but with so many people traveling for the census, other relatives were likely already staying in the upper room or an attached guest space that was built at the back of the house where Mary and Joseph lodged. When it was time for Mary to go into labor, propriety and practicality would require the men to leave the main room of the house. Assisted by a local midwife, Mary would give birth in the company of cousins and aunts.[63] Jesus would be welcomed into the world by women.

⁵¹ He has done a mighty deed with his arm;

he has scattered the proud

because of the thoughts of their hearts;

⁵² he has toppled the mighty from their thrones

and exalted the lowly.

⁵³ He has satisfied the hungry with good things

and sent the rich away empty.

⁵⁴ He has helped his servant Israel,

remembering his mercy

⁵⁵ to Abraham and his descendants forever,

just as he spoke to our ancestors.

⁵⁶ And Mary stayed with her about three months; then she returned to her home.

LUKE 2:1-7

¹ In those days a decree went out from Caesar Augustus that the whole empire should be registered. ² This first registration took place while Quirinius was governing Syria. ³ So everyone went to be registered, each to his own town.

⁴ Joseph also went up from the town of Nazareth in Galilee, to Judea, to the city of David, which is called Bethlehem, because he was of the house and family line of David, ⁵ to be registered along with Mary, who was engaged to him and was pregnant. ⁶ While they were there, the time came for her to give birth. ⁷ Then she gave birth to her firstborn son, and she wrapped him tightly in cloth and laid him in a manger, because there was no guest room available for them.

MATTHEW 2:1-18

WISE MEN VISIT THE KING

¹ After Jesus was born in Bethlehem of Judea in the days of King Herod, wise men from the east arrived in Jerusalem, ² saying, "Where is he who has been born king of the Jews? For we saw his star at its rising and have come to worship him."

³ When King Herod heard this, he was deeply disturbed, and all Jerusalem with him. ⁴ So he assembled all the chief priests and scribes of the people and asked them where the Messiah would be born.

⁵ "In Bethlehem of Judea," they told him, "because this is what was written by the prophet:

⁶ **And you, Bethlehem,** in the land of Judah,

are by no means **least among the rulers of Judah:**

Because out of you will come a ruler

who will shepherd my people Israel."

⁷ Then Herod secretly summoned the wise men and asked them the exact time the star appeared. ⁸ He sent them to Bethlehem and said, "Go and search carefully for the child. When you find him, report back to me so that I too can go and worship him."

⁹ After hearing the king, they went on their way. And there it was — the star they had seen at its rising. It led them until it came and stopped above the place where the child was. ¹⁰ When they saw the star, they were overwhelmed with joy. ¹¹ Entering the house, they saw the child with Mary his mother, and falling to their knees, they worshiped him. Then they opened their treasures and presented him with gifts: gold, frankincense, and myrrh. ¹² And being warned in a dream not to go back to Herod, they returned to their own country by another route.

THE FLIGHT INTO EGYPT

¹³ After they were gone, an angel of the Lord appeared to Joseph in a dream, saying, "Get up! Take the child and his mother, flee to Egypt, and stay there until I tell you. For Herod is about to search for the child to kill him." ¹⁴ So he got up, took the child and his mother during the night, and escaped to Egypt. ¹⁵ He stayed there until Herod's death, so that what was spoken by the Lord through the prophet might be fulfilled: **Out of Egypt I called my Son.**

THE MASSACRE OF THE INNOCENTS

¹⁶ Then Herod, when he realized that he had been outwitted by the wise men, flew into a rage. He gave orders to massacre all the boys in and around Bethlehem who were two years old and under, in keeping with the time he had learned from the wise men. ¹⁷ Then what was spoken through Jeremiah the prophet was fulfilled:

¹⁸ **A voice was heard in Ramah,**
weeping, and great mourning,
Rachel weeping for her children;
and she refused to be consoled,
because they are no more.

JOHN 19:25-27

²⁵ Standing by the cross of Jesus were his mother, his mother's sister, Mary the wife of Clopas, and Mary Magdalene. ²⁶ When Jesus saw his mother and the disciple he loved standing there, he said to his mother, "Woman, here is your son." ²⁷ Then he said to the disciple, "Here is your mother." And from that hour the disciple took her into his home.

Blessed *is she who has believed that the Lord would fulfill what he has spoken to her!*

Luke 1:45

Study Tool Synthesis

Try your hand at making your own notes and observations before flipping over to the questions for this lesson.

MEDITATION LITERATURE   *What detail drives my imagination?*

PATTERNS   *What themes or repetition do I observe?*

STORY ARRANGEMENT   *What does the biblical author say?*

DIVINE AUTHORSHIP   *What does God reveal about himself?*

CHARACTER SPEECH   *What do the women say?*

A BROKEN WORLD   *What needs redemption?*

APPLICATION   *How might this story impact my week?*

Lesson 16 Questions

1. How does a cultural understanding of hospitality practice and the arrangement of a home in the Ancient Near East change the way you think about the birth of Jesus?

2. **Mary accepts the message from the angel, even though the circumstances of her pregnancy would have brought great cultural shame upon her, even the risk of stoning. How might this experience impact her life for the long term? Do you think she recognized the great cost she would pay to follow God? What does it cost you to follow God?**

3. Before Mary has a chance to explain her situation, her cousin Elizabeth is filled with the Holy Spirit and affirms what the angel told Mary. Read more about Elizabeth in Luke 1. What does Luke tell us about her? Given the cultural priorities of the day, is she the person that you would expect God to use to first proclaim the arrival of the Messiah?

4. Compare the relationship of Ruth and Naomi to Mary and Elizabeth. What do they show us about the value of intergenerational relationships?

Ruth and Naomi

Mary and Elizabeth

5. Like Hannah, Mary sings in celebration of her miraculous conception. Look back at Hannah's song on pages 95-96. What do both women proclaim about God? How do their songs complement one another? How do both women participate in God's plan for salvation?

6. **Imagine the juxtaposition of having a group of foreign sages bring some of the most expensive gifts you've ever seen, then moments later learning that you will need to load everything onto your donkey and flee the country with your young son. What thoughts and emotions might Mary have in this situation? What does this part of the story show us about God's provision?**

7. Mary, Joseph, and Jesus escaped Bethlehem in the wake of a massacre. What story does this remind you of? How does this connection build anticipation for the deliverance Jesus will provide? How will Jesus be different?

8. We usually think of all the things that Jesus gives to us, but as a child, he received the teaching, love, and care of his mother. In what ways does Mary's mothering mirror the women we've studied so far? How does she differ?

9. The gospel of John gives a final portrait of Mary at the foot of the cross. How does Jesus provide for his mother? What does this show you about God's view of women?

10. **Given maternal and infant mortality rates at this time, the very act of birth was a battle between life and death. How does Mary courageously fight for life? Are you caught in a fight between life and death, either literally or metaphorically? How could Mary's story encourage your attitude and choices?**

Lesson 16
Prayer

The women in Bethlehem supported Mary in delivering the promised Messiah, but this isn't the first time in Scripture where we see women delivering the one who would deliver them. King David shows us how both kinds of deliverance reflect the image of God. Jesus is both a deliverer of nations, and like a midwife, our intimate, personal deliverer. At times when we don't know what to pray, the Psalms can give voice to the groanings of our heart. Read the passage below and share with God which parts resonate with you.

Psalm 22:1–5, 9–10

¹ My God, my God, why have you abandoned me?

Why are you so far from my deliverance

and from my words of groaning?

² My God, I cry by day, but you do not answer,

by night, yet I have no rest.

³ But you are holy,

enthroned on the praises of Israel.

⁴ Our ancestors trusted in you;

they trusted, and you rescued them.

⁵ They cried to you and were set free;

they trusted in you and were not disgraced.

. . .

⁹ It was you who brought me out of the womb,

making me secure at my mother's breast.

¹⁰ I was given over to you at birth;

you have been my God from my mother's womb.

Mary & Martha of Bethany

Character Portrait

Who	Sisters of Lazarus, the man whom Jesus raised from the dead
When	30–33 AD
Where	Bethany, a village just outside of Jerusalem on the West Bank

Study Tool

Patterns — *A Servant Ministry*

Servant is one of those words in Scripture that can sometimes come with a bit of baggage. As readers, we tend to bring our own cultural expectations for service, which can include the historical reality of oppression and forced servitude as well as a modern disdain for charity or handouts.

Hopefully it doesn't surprise you by now to find that God's idea of service defies ancient expectations as frequently as our own. From the beginning, we see God coming down to us, bridging the gap between our inability and his perfect holiness. In his covenants with Abraham, Moses, and David, God establishes a relationship similar to that of a feudal lord with the peasants who worked his land.[64] He promises protection and blessing, but even within an elaborate sacrificial system, he is focused on faithfulness, not payment. God walks through the animal halves, committing to Abraham that he will always foot the bill,[65] and time and time again, God refuses to forget his promise or his people, no matter how wayward they become.

In his ministry, Jesus demonstrates this same sacrifice, washing the feet of his disciples, rejecting earthly rulership, and ultimately giving his very life to establish our permanent access to God. Our service to God is an appropriate posture between creation and Creator, and yet it is remarkably motivated and modeled. We serve God in response to his unending love for us, and we understand how to serve by looking at the example of Jesus.

In the text of Scripture, service does not always indicate menial tasks like cooking or waiting on tables, but can also include leading, hosting, and providing financially. Still, it never loses the connotation of putting oneself into an inferior position.[66] Where we see women serving, we should not assume *subservience*, but rather walking in the way of Jesus, a willingness to humbly give what we have from a place of love. •

Lesson 17
Passage

Under Mary's mothering care and guidance, Jesus grows into adulthood. His earthly father, Joseph, trains him as a carpenter, and around age 30, Jesus begins a public life of ministry, calling twelve men as his inner circle of disciples. Often frustrating the religious elite, Jesus heals the sick and attracts a following of men and women who call him Rabbi.

Female Disciples

Rabbinical teaching at this time discouraged men from even having conversations at length with women, let alone teaching them. In fact, religious teaching for women was considered such a waste of time that some rabbis went as far as suggesting that educating them was worse than selling them into prostitution.[67]

Not only do we see Jesus speaking with Mary, but the phrase "to sit at the feet of" is shorthand for becoming a disciple.[68] Jesus has formally engaged Mary as his student.

Luke's version of the life of Jesus specifically highlights how women joined the disciples from the earliest stages of his ministry. Women were among the seventy-two followers Jesus sent to neighboring villages to share the good news of his coming.[69] They also served and financially provided for Jesus.[70] His closest twelve disciples may have been male, but the women were engaged and involved in critical ways.

LUKE 10:38-42

[38] While they were traveling, he entered a village, and a woman named Martha welcomed him into her home. [39] She had a sister named Mary, who also sat at the Lord's feet and was listening to what he said. [40] But Martha was distracted by her many tasks, and she came up and asked, "Lord, don't you care that my sister has left me to serve alone? So tell her to give me a hand."

[41] The Lord answered her, "Martha, Martha, you are worried and upset about many things, [42] but one thing is necessary. Mary has made the right choice, and it will not be taken away from her."

JOHN 11:1-44

LAZARUS DIES AT BETHANY

[1] Now a man was sick, Lazarus from Bethany, the village of Mary and her sister Martha. [2] Mary was the one who anointed the Lord with perfume and wiped his feet with her hair, and it was her brother Lazarus who was sick. [3] So the sisters sent a message to him: "Lord, the one you love is sick."

[4] When Jesus heard it, he said, "This sickness will not end in death but is for the glory of God, so that the Son of God may be glorified through it." [5] Now Jesus loved Martha, her sister, and Lazarus. [6] So when he heard that he was sick, he stayed two more days in the place where he was. [7] Then after that, he said to the disciples, "Let's go to Judea again."

[8] "Rabbi," the disciples told him, "just now the Jews tried to stone you, and you're going there again?"

[9] "Aren't there twelve hours in a day?" Jesus answered. "If anyone walks during the day, he doesn't stumble, because he sees the light of this world. [10] But if anyone walks during the night, he does stumble, because the light is not in him."

[11] He said this, and then he told them, "Our friend Lazarus has fallen asleep, but I'm on my way to wake him up."

[12] Then the disciples said to him, "Lord, if he has fallen asleep, he will get well."

[13] Jesus, however, was speaking about his death, but they thought he was speaking about natural sleep. [14] So Jesus then told them plainly, "Lazarus has died. [15] I'm glad for you that I wasn't there so that you may believe. But let's go to him."

[16] Then Thomas (called "Twin") said to his fellow disciples, "Let's go too so that we may die with him."

THE RESURRECTION AND THE LIFE

[17] When Jesus arrived, he found that Lazarus had already been in the tomb four days. [18] Bethany was near Jerusalem (less than two miles away). [19] Many of the Jews had come to Martha and Mary to comfort them about their brother.

20 As soon as Martha heard that Jesus was coming, she went to meet him, but Mary remained seated in the house. 21 Then Martha said to Jesus, "Lord, if you had been here, my brother wouldn't have died. 22 Yet even now I know that whatever you ask from God, God will give you."

23 "Your brother will rise again," Jesus told her.

24 Martha said to him, "I know that he will rise again in the resurrection at the last day."

25 Jesus said to her, "I am the resurrection and the life. The one who believes in me, even if he dies, will live. 26 Everyone who lives and believes in me will never die. Do you believe this?"

27 "Yes, Lord," she told him, "I believe you are the Messiah, the Son of God, who comes into the world."

JESUS SHARES THE SORROW OF DEATH

28 Having said this, she went back and called her sister Mary, saying in private, "The Teacher is here and is calling for you."

29 As soon as Mary heard this, she got up quickly and went to him. 30 Jesus had not yet come into the village but was still in the place where Martha had met him. 31 The Jews who were with her in the house consoling her saw that Mary got up quickly and went out. They followed her, supposing that she was going to the tomb to cry there.

32 As soon as Mary came to where Jesus was and saw him, she fell at his feet and told him, "Lord, if you had been here, my brother wouldn't have died!"

33 When Jesus saw her crying, and the Jews who had come with her crying, he was deeply moved in his spirit and troubled. 34 "Where have you put him?" he asked.

"Lord," they told him, "come and see."

35 Jesus wept.

36 So the Jews said, "See how he loved him!" 37 But some of them said, "Couldn't he who opened the blind man's eyes also have kept this man from dying?"

THE SEVENTH SIGN: RAISING LAZARUS FROM THE DEAD

38 Then Jesus, deeply moved again, came to the tomb. It was a cave, and a stone was lying against it. 39 "Remove the stone," Jesus said.

Martha, the dead man's sister, told him, "Lord, there is already a stench because he has been dead four days."

40 Jesus said to her, "Didn't I tell you that if you believed you would see the glory of God?"

⁴¹ So they removed the stone. Then Jesus raised his eyes and said, "Father, I thank you that you heard me. ⁴² I know that you always hear me, but because of the crowd standing here I said this, so that they may believe you sent me." ⁴³ After he said this, he shouted with a loud voice, "Lazarus, come out! " ⁴⁴ The dead man came out bound hand and foot with linen strips and with his face wrapped in a cloth. Jesus said to them, "Unwrap him and let him go."

The two passages below describe the same scene of Jesus's anointing from different perspectives.

JOHN 12:1-8

THE ANOINTING AT BETHANY

¹ Six days before the Passover, Jesus came to Bethany where Lazarus was, the one Jesus had raised from the dead. ² So they gave a dinner for him there; Martha was serving them, and Lazarus was one of those reclining at the table with him. ³ Then Mary took a pound of perfume, pure and expensive nard, anointed Jesus's feet, and wiped his feet with her hair. So the house was filled with the fragrance of the perfume.

⁴ Then one of his disciples, Judas Iscariot (who was about to betray him), said, ⁵ "Why wasn't this perfume sold for three hundred denarii and given to the poor?" ⁶ He didn't say this because he cared about the poor but because he was a thief. He was in charge of the money-bag and would steal part of what was put in it.

⁷ Jesus answered, "Leave her alone; she has kept it for the day of my burial. ⁸ For you always have the poor with you, but you do not always have me."

MARK 14:3-9

³ While he was in Bethany at the house of Simon the leper, as he was reclining at the table, a woman came with an alabaster jar of very expensive perfume of pure nard. She broke the jar and poured it on his head. ⁴ But some were expressing indignation to one another: "Why has this perfume been wasted? ⁵ For this perfume might have been sold for more than three hundred denarii and given to the poor." And they began to scold her.

⁶ Jesus replied, "Leave her alone. Why are you bothering her? She has done a noble thing for me. ⁷ You always have the poor with you, and you can do what is good for them whenever you want, but you do not always have me. ⁸ She has done what she could; she has anointed my body in advance for burial. ⁹ Truly I tell you, wherever the gospel is proclaimed in the whole world, what she has done will also be told in memory of her."

Study Tool Synthesis

Try your hand at making your own notes and observations before flipping over to the questions for this lesson.

MEDITATION LITERATURE   *What detail drives my imagination?*

PATTERNS   *What themes or repetition do I observe?*

STORY ARRANGEMENT   *What does the biblical author say?*

DIVINE AUTHORSHIP   *What does God reveal about himself?*

CHARACTER SPEECH   *What do the women say?*

A BROKEN WORLD   *What needs redemption?*

APPLICATION   *How might this story impact my week?*

Lesson 17 Questions

1. **Compare the conversations Jesus has with Martha in the first and second stories. How does the second story give us a more complete picture of Martha?**

	What Martha says to Jesus	What Jesus says to Martha	What the author tells us about their relationship	What the interaction demonstrates about their relationship
Luke 10				
John 11				

2. **Jesus affirms the value of spiritual education for women. In what ways does Jesus intellectually engage with both Mary and Martha? What does this show us about the importance of women in the church today?**

3. Jesus realigns Martha's priorities and the disciples who rebuke Mary. We see elsewhere in Scripture the importance of hospitality, service, and giving, but Jesus wants his followers to recognize the unique opportunity of his presence. How might this teaching affect your own priorities? How does it change the way you view reading the Bible?

4. Lazarus' story is a particularly famous account that we often read from a male perspective, either considering Jesus's, his disciples', or Lazarus's experiences. Did you notice anything different about the story when reading it to learn about Mary and Martha? What other stories in Scripture would you understand differently if you viewed the events through the eyes of women?

5. The extravagance of the oil Mary uses is above and beyond the common household varieties used to anoint guests.[71] Why does Mary believe this display is necessary? What does this show us about her values?

6. **Jesus allows women to touch him, though the Jewish tradition of the day forbade women from even speaking to men. Jesus makes no comment about Mary's unbound hair, though it was a display of intimacy only seen by a woman's husband. He doesn't worry about keeping up appearances, and yet he's also never inappropriate. How does Jesus's interaction with Mary and Martha honor the value of women? What modern stereotypes about women does Jesus also defy?**

7. Which of these sisters do you more closely relate to? How do their stories impact the way you view the women in your community?

8. Underline the displays of emotion that you see in these passages. How does Jesus react to them? What insight does this offer about how we should view feelings?

9. One way that Jesus teaches us about service is by receiving it graciously from women. What has this story taught you about serving or being served? What can you do this week to practice what you are learning?

Lesson 17
Prayer

In this story, we see Jesus as teacher, comforter, and friend. Which of these descriptors is most powerful for you personally? Write a prayer of thanksgiving for how Jesus has been this for you.

Photine, the Samaritan Woman*

Character Portrait

Who	A foreign woman who becomes one of the first evangelists
When	30–33 AD
Where	Jacob's well in Sychar, a town of Samaria, on the road to Galilee

Study Tool

A Broken World — *The Complications of Ancient Marriage*

A number of different interpretations of Photine's story have been taught throughout church history, but the prevailing trend is to view her as a prostitute or bed-hopping divorcee.[72] However, the cultural expectations for marriage during this time period ❶ ❹ require us to carefully consider the details included in the text so that we are not reading our agenda into Jesus's story.

First, we notice what is missing—Jesus does not indicate whether her previous husbands died or divorced her, so we cannot rule out the possibility that she lived through a number of tragedies and rejections. At the same time, six different marriages is an unusually high number. Available legal records of the time do not record more than three,[73] so this detail should pique our interest.

As we think through some of the possible reasons for Photine's many relationships, additional information about marriage in the Roman era can help. Girls were trained in household management and raised to expect marriage. Their union cemented social bonds between households in the community and created the context for legitimate children.[74] To achieve the most successful match, a young girl's male guardians would formally arrange a marriage contract that they felt would be socially and economically advantageous.[75] If her husband died, a woman had no claim on his inheritance and his family was not obligated to allow her to remain in their household. If she had no adult children to support her, she would return to her father's home with her dowry, where

Though the Bible does not offer a name for the Samaritan woman, the Catholic Church has traditionally honored her with the name Photine. I am using this personal name as a pseudonym to help us remember that she has a real identity, even if God alone knows her real name.

her family would be responsible for arranging a second marriage. A woman would need to be independently wealthy, with either a dowry or inheritance of her own, for it to be practical to remain unmarried, although a young woman with significant personal resources would also be an attractive partner for another family.[76] Because Photine was able to successfully remarry so many times, it is less likely that she had a reputation for adultery or infertility, which would make it more difficult for her family to find a willing subsequent match.[77]

Women would have several hurdles for initiating divorce. While Roman law allowed a woman to end her marriage, the rabbinical tradition forbade it. A number of complicating factors also made this less feasible or attractive. In leaving the marriage, a woman could not take her children since they officially belonged to their father's household. She would also need the support of her family for a place to live and to successfully negotiate the return of her dowry.[78]

A couple of realities might explain why Photine is currently living with a man who is not her legal husband.

The beginning of a marriage did not include standardized ceremonies the way we think of a wedding today and therefore could be ambiguous. Sometimes a wife would be sent to her new home before the marriage contract was finalized.[79] Additionally, Roman law prevented citizens from marrying any non-citizen, soldier, or even formerly enslaved person. Rabbis had similar prohibitions, including marriage restrictions for priests. For these reasons, a formalized cohabitation agreement was viewed as a morally acceptable alternative to marriage when legal structures prevented it.[80] In order to be married five times prior, Photine was likely older, which could also impact her ability and interest in arranging yet another marriage contract.

As the writer of this story, John offers two highly unusual details that hint at Photine's character. Her arrival alone midday at the well and her previous marriages give us much to consider, but don't automatically mean that she is a sinner or outcast. In order to best understand how to view her marital history, we will need to consider the rest of the details in the story. •

Lesson 18 Passage

During Jesus' ministry, he meets with a number of individuals while traveling and teaching. His lengthy dialogue with Photine, a woman from Samaria, includes the first of several "I AM" statements in John's gospel account. This Greek phrase is the same used to translate God's message to Moses in the burning bush.[81]

JOHN 4:1-42

JESUS AND THE SAMARITAN WOMAN

[1] When Jesus learned that the Pharisees had heard he was making and baptizing more disciples than John [2] (though Jesus himself was not baptizing, but his disciples were), [3] he left Judea and went again to Galilee. [4] He had to travel through Samaria; [5] so he came to a town of Samaria called Sychar near the property that Jacob had given his son Joseph. [6] Jacob's well was there, and Jesus, worn out from his journey, sat down at the well. It was about noon.

[7] A woman of Samaria came to draw water.

"Give me a drink," Jesus said to her, [8] because his disciples had gone into town to buy food.

[9] "How is it that you, a Jew, ask for a drink from me, a Samaritan woman?" she asked him. For Jews do not associate with Samaritans.

¹⁰ Jesus answered, "If you knew the gift of God, and who is saying to you, 'Give me a drink,' you would ask him, and he would give you living water."

¹¹ "Sir," said the woman, "you don't even have a bucket, and the well is deep. So where do you get this 'living water'? ¹² You aren't greater than our father Jacob, are you? He gave us the well and drank from it himself, as did his sons and livestock."

¹³ Jesus said, "Everyone who drinks from this water will get thirsty again. ¹⁴ But whoever drinks from the water that I will give him will never get thirsty again. In fact, the water I will give him will become a well of water springing up in him for eternal life."

¹⁵ "Sir," the woman said to him, "give me this water so that I won't get thirsty and come here to draw water."

¹⁶ "Go call your husband," he told her, "and come back here."

¹⁷ "I don't have a husband," she answered.

"You have correctly said, 'I don't have a husband,'" Jesus said. ¹⁸ "For you've had five husbands, and the man you now have is not your husband. What you have said is true."

¹⁹ "Sir," the woman replied, "I see that you are a prophet. ²⁰ Our ancestors worshiped on this mountain, but you Jews say that the place to worship is in Jerusalem."

²¹ Jesus told her, "Believe me, woman, an hour is coming when you will worship the Father neither on this mountain nor in Jerusalem. ²² You Samaritans worship what you do not know. We worship what we do know, because salvation is from the Jews. ²³ But an hour is coming, and is now here, when the true worshipers will worship the Father in Spirit and in truth. Yes, the Father wants such people to worship him. ²⁴ God is spirit, and those who worship him must worship in Spirit and in truth."

²⁵ The woman said to him, "I know that the Messiah is coming" (who is called Christ). "When he comes, he will explain everything to us."

²⁶ Jesus told her, "I, the one speaking to you, am he."

THE RIPENED HARVEST

²⁷ Just then his disciples arrived, and they were amazed that he was talking with a woman. Yet no one said, "What do you want?" or "Why are you talking with her?"

²⁸ Then the woman left her water jar, went into town, and told the people, ²⁹ "Come, see a man who told me everything I ever did. Could this be the Messiah?" ³⁰ They left the town and made their way to him.

An Unconventional Meetup

Several details of this meeting could have been scandalous in Jesus's time. Men who followed rabbinical instructions wouldn't even make eye contact with an unknown woman in a public place, and here we see Jesus ignoring several social rules. Not only does he dare to approach a woman in public, but he is willing to thoughtfully engage someone from an ethnic group that has been feuding with his own people for the past 500 years. We might expect a religious leader to scorn her, and yet Jesus humbles himself to ask for her help and even drinks out of her ritually defiled bucket.[82] The story's location at Jacob's well should remind us of the marriage arrangements of both Isaac and Jacob—Jesus' actions would have given people the impression that he was there to find a wife,[83] but he had an entirely different priority.

To avoid any kind of impropriety—and more practically, to avoid the heat—women would usually go to the well in groups during the morning hours. The fact that Photine is alone in the hottest part of the day signals that she is disconnected from the community of women in some way.[84] While getting water alone is not intrinsically immoral,[85] the time of day is still an unusual detail in the story and worth noting. She has to draw the water by herself.

[31] In the meantime the disciples kept urging him, "Rabbi, eat something."

[32] But he said, "I have food to eat that you don't know about."

[33] The disciples said to one another, "Could someone have brought him something to eat?"

[34] "My food is to do the will of him who sent me and to finish his work," Jesus told them. [35] "Don't you say, 'There are still four more months, and then comes the harvest'? Listen to what I'm telling you: Open your eyes and look at the fields, because they are ready for harvest. [36] The reaper is already receiving pay and gathering fruit for eternal life, so that the sower and reaper can rejoice together. [37] For in this case the saying is true: 'One sows and another reaps.' [38] I sent you to reap what you didn't labor for; others have labored, and you have benefited from their labor."

THE SAVIOR OF THE WORLD

[39] Now many Samaritans from that town believed in him because of what the woman said when she testified, "He told me everything I ever did." [40] So when the Samaritans came to him, they asked him to stay with them, and he stayed there two days. [41] Many more believed because of what he said. [42] And they told the woman, "We no longer believe because of what you said, since we have heard for ourselves and know that this really is the Savior of the world."

Study Tool Synthesis

Try your hand at making your own notes and observations before flipping over to the questions for this lesson.

MEDITATION LITERATURE *What detail drives my imagination?*

PATTERNS *What themes or repetition do I observe?*

STORY ARRANGEMENT *What does the biblical author say?*

DIVINE AUTHORSHIP *What does God reveal about himself?*

CHARACTER SPEECH *What do the women say?*

A BROKEN WORLD *What needs redemption?*

APPLICATION *How might this story impact my week?*

Lesson 18 Questions

1. Jesus does not mention sin or forgiveness when speaking with Photine, even though he directly confronts others for their sin in the gospel account of John.[86] Is the text clear about whether she is a sinner or a sufferer? What practicalities might multiple marriages have provided? What could the woman have lost? How do Jesus's words to Photine land differently for sinners and for sufferers?

2. Photine already knows a great deal about the promises of God and asks Jesus a number of questions. Circle her statements of belief and underline each question. What additional details does Jesus reveal about himself through their conversation? What does Photine do in response to the information that she learns?

3. How we view Photine's character can influence the way her questions sound in our head. In what tone of voice do you read her questions? What is the tone of Jesus's words?

4. Jesus's disciples are surprised when they return to find Jesus talking with this woman, yet the author explains that they don't use a particular Middle Eastern idiom that means, "Do you want us to get rid of her for you?"[87] An uncomfortable silence follows. How does the conversation among these men differ from Jesus's dialogue with Photine?

5. Jesus uses two analogies in this story—a spring of living water and the sower and reaper during harvest. In what ways does Photine embody both of these?

6. As an evangelist, how is Photine's testimony received? What does her story teach us about sharing Jesus's message with others?

7. One chapter prior to this, we meet a religious man named Nicodemus who visits Jesus in the middle of the night. Read his story in John 3:1–21. List the ways that Photine's story differs from Nicodemus's. What do these contrasts reveal about the character of each person? Which story resonates more with your experience?

8. Jesus not only knows Photine's personal history but also engages her intellectually. He sees her fully and speaks directly to her heart. Which of these attributes of God are attractive to you? Why?

9. In previous stories of women, we have seen individual "outsiders" join the nation of Israel, leaving their home and family behind. What plan does Jesus share with Photine? How is Photine uniquely suited to share this message with her people? What does this teach us about the value of women in spreading and teaching the message of Jesus?

10. Some interpreters have cast Photine as the archetypal sinner—flattening her story into an object lesson about how even a foolish harlot is welcome in the Kingdom of God. What can we learn from Photine when we see her as fully human? How does Jesus treat her?

Lesson 18
Prayer

List out the ways that you feel seen, heard, and known by God. Write a prayer of gratitude to the God who cares about you as a whole person.

Veronica, the Bleeding Woman*

Character Portrait

Who	An ailing woman who pursues healing from Jesus
When	30–33 AD
Where	Near the Sea of Galilee, on the way to the home of the synagogue leader, Jairus

Study Tool

Story Arrangement — *Why are there four separate accounts of Jesus's Life?*

Matthew, Mark, Luke, and John each wrote about the life and ministry of Jesus. These four books in our Bible have different audiences and thematic goals that affect what each author includes and how the text is arranged. By comparing their perspectives, we can see which details are prominently repeated. We also find different vantage points for key moments. Today's story was significant enough that three of the four gospel writers decided to include it. We will read all three versions, including a slightly longer version of Mark's gospel to understand the context for Veronica's story. ●

*As in the last lesson, we will use the Catholic name, Veronica, for the bleeding woman since the Bible does not offer a name for her.

Lesson 19 Passage

Throughout his ministry, Jesus travels and performs many miraculous healings. He restores sight and mobility, turns water to wine, exorcizes demons, and raises the dead to life—all while sharing hints of his identity through teaching and storytelling.

MATTHEW 9:20-22

20 Just then, a woman who had suffered from bleeding for twelve years approached from behind and touched the end of his robe, 21 for she said to herself, "If I can just touch his robe, I'll be made well."

22 Jesus turned and saw her. "Have courage, daughter," he said. "Your faith has saved you." And the woman was made well from that moment.

MARK 5:21-43

21 When Jesus had crossed over again by boat to the other side, a large crowd gathered around him while he was by the sea. 22 One of the synagogue leaders, named Jairus, came, and when he saw Jesus, he fell at his feet 23 and begged him earnestly, "My little daughter is dying. Come and lay your hands on her so that she can get well and live." 24 So Jesus went with him, and a large crowd was following and pressing against him.

25 Now a woman suffering from bleeding for twelve years 26 had endured much under many doctors. She had spent everything she had and was not helped at all. On the contrary, she became worse. 27 Having heard about Jesus, she came up behind him in the crowd and touched his clothing. 28 For she said, "If I just touch his clothes, I'll be made well." 29 Instantly her flow of blood ceased, and she sensed in her body that she was healed of her affliction.

30 Immediately Jesus realized that power had gone out from him. He turned around in the crowd and said, "Who touched my clothes?"

31 His disciples said to him, "You see the crowd pressing against you, and yet you say, 'Who touched me?'"

32 But he was looking around to see who had done this. 33 The woman, with fear and trembling, knowing what had happened to her, came and fell down before him, and told him the whole truth. 34 "Daughter," he said to her, "your faith has saved you. Go in peace and be healed from your affliction."

35 While he was still speaking, people came from the synagogue leader's house and said, "Your daughter is dead. Why bother the teacher anymore?"

36 When Jesus overheard what was said, he told the synagogue leader, "Don't be afraid. Only believe." 37 He did not let anyone accompany him except Peter, James, and John, James's brother. 38 They came to the leader's house, and he saw a commotion — people weeping and wailing loudly. 39 He went in and said to them, "Why are you making a commotion and weeping? The child is not dead but asleep." 40 They laughed at him, but he put them all outside. He took the child's father, mother, and those who were with him, and entered the place where the child was. 41 Then he took the child by the hand and said to her, "Talitha koum" (which is translated, "Little girl, I say to you, get up"). 42 Immediately the girl got up and began to walk. (She was twelve years old.) At this they were utterly astounded. 43 Then he gave them strict orders that no one should know about this and told them to give her something to eat.

42b While he was going, the crowds were nearly crushing him. 43 A woman suffering from bleeding for twelve years, who had spent all she had on doctors and yet could not be healed by any, 44 approached from behind and touched the end of his robe. Instantly her bleeding stopped.

45 "Who touched me?" Jesus asked.

When they all denied it, Peter said, "Master, the crowds are hemming you in and pressing against you."

46 "Someone did touch me," said Jesus. "I know that power has gone out from me." 47 When the woman saw that she was discovered, she came trembling and fell down before him. In the presence of all the people, she declared the reason she had touched him and how she was instantly healed. 48 "Daughter," he said to her, "your faith has saved you. Go in peace."

Why was bleeding considered "impure"?

Leviticus records a lengthy collection of laws for the Israelites to follow in order to draw near to God. Because God is immeasurably holy—so full of goodness, life, and light—only those who are unblemished in any way can safely come close to him without suffering harm. As with the sun in the sky, we simply cannot withstand direct contact in our imperfect human state. The design of the tabernacle and temple restricted access to God to protect his people from a holiness so pure it could kill them on the spot. The Israelite Law gave instructions for how to become temporarily pure so that a person could worship in the presence of God.[88]

Some of the Levitical law gives guidance related to morality, while other sections provide regulations surrounding ritual purity or cleanliness. Careful distinction between ritual purity and moral purity is important because cleanliness should not be conflated with a person's value or goodness.[89] Simply by virtue of being human, all people experienced periods of uncleanliness and needed to offer specific sacrifices to become clean again. So, for example, touching someone who was sick or dying was not morally wrong, but would render a person ritually unclean until they made the proper sacrifice.

The point of the Law was never to assign rank or status, like some competition for cleanliness. Instead, it revealed how desperately we all need intervention. Even if we could follow the moral purity laws perfectly, our post-Eden bodies could never remain ritually clean. Nearness to God under the Law required continuous, habitual sacrifice. Permanent closeness would need something more.

Regulations in the Law surrounding childbirth and menstruation were based on this understanding of God's holiness and the people's need for ritual cleanliness.[90] Each time a woman had her period, ritual purity practices acknowledged her blood as a life lost.[91] This connection between blood and death made the woman and anyone who touched her temporarily impure. After making the appropriate sacrifices, they could become clean once again.

A woman who bled continuously, however, would have no opportunity to become clean. She could not worship at the temple and might be shunned by others who viewed her perpetual uncleanliness as contagion. Her life was marked by a constant reminder of death and separation.

The woman, with fear and trembling, knowing what had happened to her, came and fell down before him, and told him the whole truth.

Mark 5:33

Study Tool Synthesis

Try your hand at making your own notes and observations before flipping over to the questions for this lesson.

MEDITATION LITERATURE   *What detail drives my imagination?*

PATTERNS   *What themes or repetition do I observe?*

STORY ARRANGEMENT   *What does the biblical author say?*

DIVINE AUTHORSHIP   *What does God reveal about himself?*

CHARACTER SPEECH   *What do the women say?*

A BROKEN WORLD   *What needs redemption?*

APPLICATION   *How might this story impact my week?*

Lesson 19 Questions

1. Consider the circumstances of Veronica's life. She appears in the crowd without the protection of a husband or father to advocate on her behalf, so we might assume that she has either never married or was divorced. Even if she had inheritance or a returned dowry, the biblical author explains that she depleted everything in her efforts to find treatment.[92] **What other details in the story attest to Veronica's desperation? What details affirm her faith?**

2. Imagine what life would be like if you had gone more than a decade without being allowed to touch another person. In what ways can you relate to this woman's loneliness?

3. In each of the gospel accounts, Veronica's story is sandwiched between the first and second half of another story. The story of Jairus and his ailing daughter is included here in Mark's version, but can also be found by looking up the surrounding verses in Matthew and Luke. Compare and contrast these two stories. What themes connect the two? Though Jairus' situation was urgent, what does it mean for Veronica that Jesus would take time to engage her?

Veronica

Jairus's Daughter

4. Why might Veronica prefer to remain hidden? What areas of shame, sin, or suffering would you prefer to keep hidden? By inviting her out of the crowd, what does Jesus offer Veronica?

5. Veronica is the only woman Jesus ever referred to as "Daughter" in the pages of Scripture.[93] Considering the family structures of the day, ❶ ❹ what does this relationship imply? What does it mean to you that God calls believers his sons and daughters?

6. **When an unclean person came too close to God in the Old Testament, they would die. But nearness to Jesus offers life. Veronica's touch should have made Jesus unclean, and yet somehow he made her clean.[94] How is Jesus able to do this? What hints of Passover do you see in Veronica's story?**

7. Purity laws were designed to protect God's people from his holiness, but sadly became weaponized against marginalized people. Religious leaders avoided and looked down upon those who were unclean, and the community often assumed that illness was a punishment for the person's sin.[95] How is Jesus's reaction different? How does this offer hope to someone who may have suffered social rejection, even within a church?

8. Read Hebrews 4:14-16. A high priest was able to offer sacrifices to declare a person clean, but he could not actually heal. In what ways does Veronica's story affirm Jesus as a better high priest than Moses or any who came after him?

9. Many of Jesus's disciples had a healing experience, including Mary Magdalene, who we will meet in the next lesson. What does it mean to be healed? How does this experience change someone? Where can we find hope when our suffering is not met with the kind of healing we would like?

10. **Israel could only become ritually clean enough to temporarily endure the holy presence of God through the sacrifice of animals. But Jesus' death and resurrection was such a powerful sacrifice that we could be made permanently clean. What would that mean for Veronica? What does that mean for you today?**

Lesson 19
Prayer

List the attributes of Jesus that you observe in this story. Write a prayer of adoration for our God who is both Priest and Physician. Go back one more time to your list from Lesson 8 and share one new thing you have learned about Jesus with them this week.

Mary Magdalene & the Resurrection Witnesses

Character Portrait

Mary Magdalene	A disciple of Jesus from the fishing village of Magdala in Galilee who had been saved from seven demons; the first person to see Jesus resurrected
When	33 AD
Where	Golgotha, the place of the skull, and Joseph of Arimathea's family tomb

Joanna	A disciple and financial supporter of Jesus who was married to Herod's household manager, Chuza
Mary of Clopas	Jesus' aunt, married to Clopas, the brother of Joseph of Nazareth
Mary the Mother of James and Joseph	A disciple of Jesus
Mother Mary	The mother of Jesus and at least four other sons and two daughters, including the authors of the New Testament books of James and Jude
Salome	A disciple of Jesus, possibly the same woman mentioned as the mother to the sons of Zebedee, James and John

Study Tool
Meditation — *Reading and Re-Reading*

Today's reading is a synthesis of the Bible's climactic story from the four gospel writers—the death and resurrection of Jesus. Some sections repeat and each writer adds different key details. If you've been a Christian for a long time, this story may feel so familiar that you are tempted to skim through it. But, slow down. Deeply engage your imagination. Make time to marvel at how God restores creation. •

Lesson 20 Passage

In addition to Jesus' inner circle of twelve disciples, a number of women traveled with him, supporting his work in practical ways and learning alongside the men. The gospel accounts agree that a group of women witnessed Jesus' death, burial, and resurrection, although each writer names a different set of women depending on who would have been familiar to his particular readers.[96] As Jesus takes his final breaths on earth, these six women—and possibly others—witness his crucifixion.

JOHN 19:25-27

25 Standing by the cross of Jesus were his mother, his mother's sister, Mary the wife of Clopas, and Mary Magdalene. 26 When Jesus saw his mother and the disciple he loved standing there, he said to his mother, "Woman, here is your son." 27 Then he said to the disciple, "Here is your mother." And from that hour the disciple took her into his home.

More about Mary Magdalene

The fact that Mary Magdalene had been possessed by demons suggests that she was either never married or would have been rejected or divorced by her husband. Her condition itself might have prevented her from the regular duties a wife needed to provide in her household.[97]

MATTHEW 27:45-56

45 From noon until three in the afternoon, darkness came over the whole land. 46 About three in the afternoon Jesus cried out with a loud voice, "Elí, Elí, lemá sabachtháni?" that is, "My God, my God, why have you abandoned me?"

47 When some of those standing there heard this, they said, "He's calling for Elijah."

48 Immediately one of them ran and got a sponge, filled it with sour wine, put it on a stick, and offered him a drink. 49 But the rest said, "Let's see if Elijah comes to save him."

50 But Jesus cried out again with a loud voice and gave up his spirit. 51 Suddenly, the curtain of the sanctuary was torn in two from top to bottom, the earth quaked, and the rocks were split. 52 The tombs were also opened and many bodies of the saints who had fallen asleep were raised. 53 And they came out of the tombs after his resurrection, entered the holy city, and appeared to many.

54 When the centurion and those with him, who were keeping watch over Jesus, saw the earthquake and the things that had happened, they were terrified and said, "Truly this man was the Son of God!"

55 Many women who had followed Jesus from Galilee and looked after him were there, watching from a distance. 56 Among them were Mary Magdalene, Mary the mother of James and Joseph, and the mother of Zebedee's sons.

MARK 15:40-41

40 There were also women watching from a distance. Among them were Mary Magdalene, Mary the mother of James the younger and of Joses, and Salome. 41 In Galilee these women followed him and took care of him. Many other women had come up with him to Jerusalem.

LUKE 23:50-56

50 There was a good and righteous man named Joseph, a member of the Sanhedrin, 51 who had not agreed with their plan and action. He was from Arimathea, a Judean town, and was looking forward to the kingdom of God. 52 He approached Pilate and asked for Jesus's body. 53 Taking it down, he wrapped it in fine linen and placed it in a tomb cut into the rock, where no one had ever been placed. 54 It was the preparation day, and the Sabbath was about to begin. 55 The women who had come with him from Galilee followed along and observed the tomb and how his body was placed. 56 Then they returned and prepared spices and perfumes. And they rested on the Sabbath according to the commandment.

Women and the Body of Jesus

Women in Jesus's day were responsible for gathering and preparing herbs and spices for feasts and ceremonies. In addition to their own monthly cycle, their role in delivering babies and preparing bodies for burial required a willingness to be regularly unclean. It also positions them as an essential presence for both the beginning and the end of life.[98]

MATTHEW 27:57-66

THE BURIAL OF JESUS

57 When it was evening, a rich man from Arimathea named Joseph came, who himself had also become a disciple of Jesus. 58 He approached Pilate and asked for Jesus's body. Then Pilate ordered that it be released. 59 So Joseph took the body, wrapped it in clean, fine linen, 60 and placed it in his new tomb, which he had cut into the rock. He left after rolling a great stone against the entrance of the tomb. 61 Mary Magdalene and the other Mary were seated there, facing the tomb.

THE CLOSELY GUARDED TOMB

62 The next day, which followed the preparation day, the chief priests and the Pharisees gathered before Pilate 63 and said, "Sir, we remember that while this deceiver was still alive he said, 'After three days I will rise again.' 64 So give orders that the tomb be made secure until the third day. Otherwise, his disciples may come, steal him, and tell the people, 'He has been raised from the dead,' and the last deception will be worse than the first."

65 "Take guards," Pilate told them. "Go and make it as secure as you know how." 66 They went and secured the tomb by setting a seal on the stone and placing the guards.

MATTHEW 28:1-10

RESURRECTION MORNING

1 After the Sabbath, as the first day of the week was dawning, Mary Magdalene and the other Mary went to view the tomb.

2 There was a violent earthquake, because an angel of the Lord descended from heaven and approached the tomb. He rolled back the stone and was sitting on it. 3 His appearance was like lightning, and his clothing was as white as snow. 4 The guards were so shaken by fear of him that they became like dead men.

5 The angel told the women, "Don't be afraid, because I know you are looking for Jesus who was crucified. 6 He is not here. For he has risen, just as he said. Come and see the place where he lay. 7 Then go quickly and tell his disciples, 'He has risen from the dead and indeed he is going ahead of you to Galilee; you will see him there.' Listen, I have told you."

8 So, departing quickly from the tomb with fear and great joy, they ran to tell his disciples the news. 9 Just then Jesus met them and said, "Greetings!" They came up, took hold of his feet, and worshiped him. 10 Then Jesus told them,"Do not be afraid. Go and tell my brothers to leave for Galilee, and they will see me there."

Essential Eyewitnesses

Women were not allowed to serve as official witnesses in Jewish court of law. Ancient prejudice assumed that they were too emotional and less capable of thoughtful introspection and response than men.[99] Not only are the women a "less reliable" source, but appearing first to them also bucks against the idea that God always privileges men over women.[100] Even though those outside of the young Christian church may have found the witness of women problematic, the community itself respected their testimony.[101] These women were the eyewitnesses, which allowed Matthew, Mark, Luke, and John to know and record the events surrounding Jesus's death and resurrection.[102]

LUKE 24:1-12

[1] On the first day of the week, very early in the morning, they came to the tomb, bringing the spices they had prepared. [2] They found the stone rolled away from the tomb. [3] They went in but did not find the body of the Lord Jesus. [4] While they were perplexed about this, suddenly two men stood by them in dazzling clothes. [5] So the women were terrified and bowed down to the ground.

"Why are you looking for the living among the dead?" asked the men. [6] "He is not here, but he has risen! Remember how he spoke to you when he was still in Galilee, [7] saying, 'It is necessary that the Son of Man be betrayed into the hands of sinful men, be crucified, and rise on the third day'?" [8] And they remembered his words.

[9] Returning from the tomb, they reported all these things to the Eleven and to all the rest. [10] Mary Magdalene, Joanna, Mary the mother of James, and the other women with them were telling the apostles these things. [11] But these words seemed like nonsense to them, and they did not believe the women. [12] Peter, however, got up and ran to the tomb. When he stooped to look in, he saw only the linen cloths. So he went away, amazed at what had happened.

More about Joanna

Luke recognizes Joanna as one of many women healed by Jesus early in his preaching ministry[103] who followed as one of his disciples.[104] As the wife of Chuza, Joanna would have had a higher social status than many of the other disciples. But following Jesus meant leaving her life of comforts to commune with the poor and outcast of society. Her former social circle would look down on her new friends and ordinary Galileans would have despised those social elites.[105] Some identify her as Junia, a prominent apostle mentioned in the letter to the Romans, suggesting that Joanna used a Greek name during her missionary travels later in life.[106]

JOHN 20:1-18

[1] On the first day of the week Mary Magdalene came to the tomb early, while it was still dark. She saw that the stone had been removed from the tomb. [2] So she went running to Simon Peter and to the other disciple, the one Jesus loved, and said to them, "They've taken the Lord out of the tomb, and we don't know where they've put him!"

[3] At that, Peter and the other disciple went out, heading for the tomb. [4] The two were running together, but the other disciple outran Peter and got to the tomb first. [5] Stooping down, he saw the linen cloths lying there, but he did not go in. [6] Then, following him, Simon Peter also came. He entered the tomb and saw the linen cloths lying there. [7] The wrapping that had been on his head was not lying with the linen cloths but was folded up in a separate place by itself. [8] The other disciple, who had reached the tomb first, then also went in, saw, and believed. [9] For they did not yet understand the Scripture that he must rise from the dead. [10] Then the disciples returned to the place where they were staying.

MARY MAGDALENE SEES THE RISEN LORD

[11] But Mary stood outside the tomb, crying. As she was crying, she stooped to look into the tomb. [12] She saw two angels in white sitting where Jesus's body had been lying, one at the head and the other at the feet. [13] They said to her, "Woman, why are you crying?"

"Because they've taken away my Lord," she told them, "and I don't know where they've put him."

[14] Having said this, she turned around and saw Jesus standing there, but she did not know it was Jesus. [15] "Woman," Jesus said to her, "why are you crying? Who is it that you're seeking?"

Supposing he was the gardener, she replied, "Sir, if you've carried him away, tell me where you've put him, and I will take him away."

[16] Jesus said to her, "Mary."

Turning around, she said to him in Aramaic, "'Rabboni!'" — which means "Teacher."

[17] "Don't cling to me," Jesus told her, "since I have not yet ascended to the Father. But go to my brothers and tell them that I am ascending to my Father and your Father, to my God and your God."

[18] Mary Magdalene went and announced to the disciples, "I have seen the Lord!" And she told them what he had said to her.

Study Tool Synthesis

Try your hand at making your own notes and observations before flipping over to the questions for this lesson.

MEDITATION LITERATURE *What detail drives my imagination?*

PATTERNS *What themes or repetition do I observe?*

STORY ARRANGEMENT *What does the biblical author say?*

DIVINE AUTHORSHIP *What does God reveal about himself?*

CHARACTER SPEECH *What do the women say?*

A BROKEN WORLD *What needs redemption?*

APPLICATION *How might this story impact my week?*

Lesson 20 Questions

1. **Circle or highlight every time a woman is mentioned in these stories. Where are the disciples? How do the cultural expectations for women give them unique access to Jesus's last moments?**

2. What details do the authors give us about the women's faith and commitment?

3. **Who does Mary Magdalene first think Jesus is? What does this identity remind you of? What happened the last time we read about a man and a woman in a garden?**

4. Once she recognizes Jesus, what does Mary Magdalene call him? What is the significance of this name for her personally? How is it significant for you?

5. Women's testimony was not recognized in the Roman court of law,[107] and yet Jesus chose women as the first to witness and share the good news of his resurrection. What does it mean to you that Jesus believes women?

6. Mary becomes an apostle to the apostles; she is among a number of women who speak the truth about Jesus's resurrection.[108] **What does her role show us about the importance of women's perspectives? How might Mary and the other female witnesses have impacted the early church?**

7. Luke tells us that several of the women who attended Jesus in death also funded his ministry. List three ways Jesus could have self-funded (the wilder, the better!). What does his reliance on women teach us?

8. Few women in Scripture formally take on roles in public society that are outside of the cultural norm (although we do see examples in Deborah, Miriam, and other prophetesses we have not studied, like Huldah and Anna), but all of the women in our study work within their position in society to affect significant change in God's narrative.[109] In what ways does your own life align with or defy cultural expectations? How are you wielding your influence for the good of God's kingdom?

9. Many of the women in the Old Testament are described in terms of their beauty and childbearing fruitfulness, but Jesus prioritizes spiritual fruitfulness. Inclusion in the kingdom of Israel was marked by circumcision but now would be replaced with gender-inclusive baptism.[110] What does that mean for you?

10. Adam's first response to Eve was to proclaim that she is "same of the same." In what ways were these women "same of the same" with the male disciples? How were they distinct? How did they complement one another as strategic partners?

Lesson 20
Prayer

From Mary's womb to the empty tomb, Jesus emerges onto the scene and changes everything. He is the son of Eve who crushes the serpent's head, the promised King of Israel who establishes his throne forever. But he is a different kind of ruler, one who lays down his life so that we might find flourishing as daughters and sons of God. By him our souls are secured for eternity, even as we endure the sin and suffering of this world. As you read Romans 8, write a prayer of thanksgiving for Jesus' sacrifice and share your longing for a final redemption.

Romans 8:22-23

22 For we know that the whole creation

has been groaning together with labor pains until now.

23 Not only that, but we ourselves

who have the Spirit as the firstfruits —

we also groan within ourselves,

eagerly waiting for adoption,

the redemption of our bodies.

Thematic Recap

In Part Four, we see women engaged directly with the presence of God in the person of Jesus. As we consider the themes in this section, notice the impact of watching women interacting with God himself in human form. Which of these themes feel most personal? How has encountering Jesus changed you?

About God	About Womanhood	About Myself
Receives care from women	Intergenerational friendships	
Invests in the spiritual development of women	Loving and sacrificial service	
Knows us intimately	Learning from Jesus	
Cleanses us from all impurity	Hope in God's healing	
Believes women	Essential eyewitnesses	

Conclusion: A Sending Prayer

Here we stand together at the empty tomb. We've walked a mile in the shoes of biblical women, and it still is not enough. There are so many more women in Scripture to understand. So much more to say about the ones we did meet. But they did teach us a lot—about ourselves, our relationships, our work, and our God.

Women in the Bible do things that women are uniquely qualified to do. They come from all walks of life, bestowed with a diversity of skills, capacity, and access to do the work that God has prepared for them. God values them as women. He invites them to join him *as women*. In their beautiful faces we see a reflection of the Son, and his greatness shines through their stories.

I hope that this study has helped you reflect more deeply on what it means to be a woman. I hope you saw yourself in the pages of Scripture, surrounded by so great a cloud of witnesses.

But most importantly, I hope that reading about these brave and beloved women made you hungry for the rest of God's incredible story. I hope it grew in you a longing to devour the Bread of Life, the Word made flesh, a body, broken for you.

I leave you now with a prayer.

May you seek wisdom like Abigail and Mary of Bethany.
May you train up the next generation like Leah and Bathsheba.
May you use your advantage to speak up for the voiceless like Esther and Ruth.
May you rejoice in God's blessing like Mary and Hannah.
May you trust in God's deliverance like Rahab and Veronica.

May you guard against harmful messages about women—
both those that imply subservience
and those that demand you hustle—
And instead proclaim, "I have seen the Lord."

All the days of your life.

Amen.

Acknowledgements

All my appreciation and thanks to the following—

Ruth Buchanan and Lucy Crabtree for brilliant editing.

Reagan Lewis for taking a chance on me.

Brian Colmery and Scott Mehl for engaging with me as a ministry partner and an intellectual peer as well as providing access to books and a space to work at the church.

Cynthia Storrs for invaluable wisdom and ministry brainstorming.

Jacy for truly corralling me in this new endeavor and for elevating my words into a work of art.

And of course to Phil for holding all the pieces together, making me heaps of coffee, engaging my nerdom, fighting my demons, thinking I could run the world, and never ever ever ever letting me give up on the dream.

Bibliography

Except where specifically noted, all dates for the character profiles are attributed to the following sources:

Hill, Andrew E. and John H. Walton. *A Survey of The Old Testament.* Grand Rapids, MI: Zondervan Publishing House, 2009.

Richter, Sandra L. *The Epic of Eden: A Christian Entry into The Old Testament.* Downers Grove, IL: IVP Academic, 2008. 108–110.

Broad date ranges are included prior to the Kingdom period to account for differences in dating methodologies.

INTRODUCTION

Content for the introduction is synthesized from the following resources:

Bailey, Kenneth E. *Jesus Through Middle Eastern Eyes: Cultural Studies in the Gospels.* Downers Grove, IL: IVP Academic, 2008.

Barber, Elizabeth Wayland. *Women's Work: The First 20,000 Years—Women, Cloth, and Society in Early Times.* New York: W. W. Norton & Company, 1995.

Ebeling, Jennie R. *Women's Lives in Biblical Times.* New York: T&T Clark International, 2010.

Jeffers, James S. *The Greco-Roman World of the New Testament Era: Exploring the Background of Early Christianity.* Downers Grove, IL: InterVarsity Press, 1999.

Reeder, Caryn A. *The Samaritan Woman's Story: Reconsidering John 4 after #ChurchToo.* Downers Grove: IL, IVP Academic, 2022.

Richter, Sandra L. *The Epic of Eden: A Christian Entry into The Old Testament.* Downers Grove, IL: IVP Academic, 2008.

Endnotes

1. Proverbs 31:10

2. Genesis 1:28

3. 1 Timothy 5:14, Titus 2:5

4. 2 Timothy 1:5

5. Proverbs 31:1

EVE

6. Tim Mackie, Jon Collins, and Carissa Quinn, "06: Literature for a Lifetime," October 18, 2021, in. *The Paradigm*, produced by BibleProject, podcast,.00:55:35, https://bibleproject.com/podcast/literature-lifetime/.

7. Sandra L. Richter, *The Epic of Eden: A Christian Entry into The Old Testament*. (Downers Grove, IL: IVP Academic, 2008), 108–110.

SARAH

8. Richter, *The Epic of Eden*, 117.

LEAH

Name meanings as listed on the family tree in this section come from the following source:

Walton, John H. *Chronological and Background Charts of the Old Testament, Revised and Expanded*. Grand Rapids, MI: Zondervan Academic, 1994.

9. "Reuben's Mandrakes," *Ligonier Ministries*, March 27, 2007, https://www.ligonier.org/learn/devotionals/reubens-mandrakes.

10. Alastair Roberts, "The Family of Abraham: Part 20—Mandrakes and Poplar Rods," April 4, 2019 in *Adversaria Videos and Podcasts*, podcast, 1:02:40. https://adversariapodcast.com/2019/04/04/the-family-of-abraham-part-20-mandrakes-and-poplar-rods/.

11. Tamar Kadari, "Leah: Midrash and Aggadah," *Jewish Women's Archive: Shalvi/Hyman Encyclopedia of Jewish Women*. December 31, 1999. https://jwa.org/encyclopedia/article/leah-midrash-and-aggadah.

RACHEL

12. Elizabeth W. Barber, *Women's Work: The First 20,000 Years, Women, Cloth, and Society in Early Times*, (New York: W. W. Norton & Company, 1995), 287–289.

13. Jacqueline E. Lapsley, *Whispering the Word: Hearing Women's Stories in The Old Testament*, (Louisville: Westminster John Knox Press, 2005), 24.

14. Lapsley, *Whispering the Word*, 25–29.

15. See Psalm 11:7, Psalm 146:6–8, Isaiah 5:16, Micah 6:8, Luke 11:42

TAMAR

16. Richter, *The Epic of Eden*, 31.; Deuteronomy 25:5–10

17. Tikva Frymer-Kensky, "Tamar: Bible," *Jewish Women's Archive: Shalvi/Hyman Encyclopedia of Jewish Women*. December 31, 1999. https://jwa.org/encyclopedia/article/tamar-bible

18. Alastair Roberts, "Hero's Theme," *Theopolis*, September 27, 2016. https://theopolisinstitute.com/18704-2/

19. Elyse Fitzpatrick and Eric Schumacher, *Worthy: Celebrating the Value of Women*, (Bethany House Publishers, 2020), 129–130.

20. Richter, The Epic of Eden, 33.

INTERLUDE: SEEING THROUGH THE EYES OF A MOTHER

21. Matthew 23:37

22. Isaiah 49:15

MIRIAM

23. John McKinley, "Necessary Allies—God as ezer, Woman as ezer" (Recorded session, 67th Annual Meeting of the Evangelical Theological Society, Atlanta, November 18, 2015).

24. Lapsley, *Whispering the Word*, 73–74.

25. Lapsley, *Whispering the Word*, 72.

26. Tim Mackie, *Themes: Holy Spirit*, Jon Collins, BibleProject, accessed February 14, 2022, video, 00:04:11, https://bibleproject.com/explore/video/holy-spirit/.

27. Aimee Byrd, *Recovering from Biblical Manhood & Womanhood: How the Church Needs to Rediscover Her Purpose*, (Grand Rapids: Zondervan, 2020), 75.

RAHAB

28. Romans 3:23, 5:12–14

Endnotes

RAHAB, Continued

29. Phyllis Bird, "'To Play the Harlot': An Inquiry into an Old Testament Metaphor," in *Gender and Difference in Ancient Israel*, ed. Peggy Lynne Day, (Minneapolis: Fortress Press, 2010), 77–79.

30. Leviticus 19:29, 21:9

31. Richard Bauckham, *Gospel Women: Studies of the Named Women in the Gospels*, (Grand Rapids, MI: William B. Eerdmans Publishing Company, 2003), 35–36.

32. Bauckham, Gospel Women, 44.

DEBORAH & JAEL

33. Susan Niditch, "Eroticism and Death in the Tale of Jael," in *Gender and Difference in Ancient Israel*, ed. Peggy Lynne Day (Minneapolis: Fortress Press, 2010), 46–48, 50.

34. Jacob L. Wright, "Jael's Identities," in *War, Memory, and National Identity in the Hebrew Bible*, (Cambridge: Cambridge University Press, 2020), 222–236, https://doi.org/10.1017/9781108691512.016.; Judges 1:16

35. 1 Timothy 5:1–2

36. Titus 2:2–5

NAOMI & RUTH

37. 2 Timothy 3:16–17

38. Andrew E. Hill and John H. Walton, *A Survey of The Old Testament*, (Grand Rapids, MI: Zondervan Publishing House, 2009), 26–27.

39. Bauckham. *Gospel Women*, 9.

40. Kenneth E. Bailey, *Jesus through Middle Eastern Eyes: Cultural Studies in the Gospels*, (Downers Grove, IL: IVP Academic, 2008), 40.

41. Lapsley, *Whispering the Word*, 94.

42. Alastair Roberts, "Why We Should Jettison the 'Strong Female Character,'" *Mere Orthodoxy* (blog), April 16, 2016, https://mereorthodoxy.com/why-we-should-jettison-the-strong-female-character.

43. Fitzpatrick and Schumacher, *Worthy*, 141.

HANNAH

44. This concept has been discussed by Alastair Roberts in a number of contexts.

45. 1 Samuel 16:7, these words are spoken by the LORD to Hannah's son, the prophet Samuel.

46. The explanation for a Nazirite vow can be found in Numbers 6:1–21.

47. 1 Samuel 2:21

48. Fitzpatrick and Schumacher, *Worthy*, 112–113.

ABIGAIL

49. Leviticus 19:33–34

50. Philip J. King and Lawrence E. Stager, *Life in Biblical Israel*, (Louisville: Westminster John Knox Press, 2001), 61–62.

51. Fitzpatrick and Schumacher, *Worthy*, 131.

BATHSHEBA

52. Richter, *The Epic of Eden*, 98.

53. See Deuteronomy 17:17

54. Information in this section is synthesized from two sources, which summarize harem practices over a large time span and in several different empires:

"Harem," Encyclopedia Britannica, accessed February 24, 2022, https://www.britannica.com/topic/harem.

"Harems," Encyclopedia of Sex and Gender: Culture Society History, accessed February 24, 2022, https://www.encyclopedia.com/social-sciences/encyclopedias-almanacs-transcripts-and-maps/harems.

55. Matthew 1:5

56. 1 Kings 10:23

VASHTI & ESTHER

The date used in these character portraits presumes that Ahasuerus is the historical Xerxes of Persia; Sandra L. Richter in *The Epic of Eden* gives the book an earlier date of 587-520 BC.

57. Hill and Walton, *A Survey*, 22.

58. Hill and Walton, *A Survey*, 350–351

Endnotes

59. "Ten Lost Tribes of Israel," *Encyclopedia Britannica*, accessed February 25, 2022, https://www.britannica.com/topic/Ten-Lost-Tribes-of-Israel.

60. Hill and Walton, *A Survey*, 351.

INTERLUDE: HEROINES, SINNERS, AND SUFFERERS

61. *The Wizard of Oz*, directed by Victor Fleming (1939; Beverly Hills: Metro-Goldwyn-Mayer, 2005), DVD.

MOTHER MARY & ELIZABETH

62. Bailey, *Middle Eastern Eyes*, 26.

63. Bailey, *Middle Eastern Eyes*, 34–35.

MARY & MARTHA OF BETHANY

64. A more historically relevant term for this arrangement is that of suzerain and vassal; however, I have chosen a different analogy only for the sake of clarity.

65. Genesis 15:1–20 follows a common model for legal contracts. Typically, the two parties in the agreement would walk through the animals together to suggest that if either breaks the contract, they should be cut in two like the animals. However, in God's covenant with Abraham, God walks through alone, declaring that he will pay the penalty for any breach.

66. Bauckham, *Gospel Women*,164.

67. Fitzpatrick and Schumacher, *Worthy*, 162.

68. Fitzpatrick and Schumacher, *Worthy*, 167.

69. Luke 10:1–20; Bauckham. *Gospel Women*, 112.

70. Luke 8:1–3, Mark 15:40–41

71. Fitzpatrick and Schumacher, *Worthy*, 173.

PHOTINE

72. Caryn A. Reeder, *The Samaritan Woman's Story: Reconsidering John 4 after #ChurchToo.* (Downers Grove, IL: IVP Academic, 2022), 19–96. Part One of this book traces the interpretations of highly influential church leaders from the early church to today, noting their relative differences in characterizing this woman.

73. Reeder, *The Samaritan Woman's Story*, 149.

74. Reeder, *The Samaritan Woman's Story*, 129 and 148.

75. Reeder, *The Samaritan Woman's Story*, 136.

76. Reeder, *The Samaritan Woman's Story*, 125 and 143.

77. Reeder, *The Samaritan Woman's Story*, 150.

78. Reeder, *The Samaritan Woman's Story*, 145 and 148.

79. Reeder, *The Samaritan Woman's Story*, 134–135.

80. Reeder, *The Samaritan Woman's Story*, 137–138.

81. Bailey, *Middle Eastern Eyes*, 211; Exodus 3:14.

82. Bailey, *Middle Eastern Eyes*, 203–205.

83. Fitzpatrick and Schumacher, *Worthy*, 161.

84. Bailey, *Middle Eastern Eyes*, 202.

85. Reeder, *The Samaritan Woman's Story*, 162.

86. Reeder, *The Samaritan Woman's Story*, 5.

87. Bailey, *Middle Eastern Eyes*, 212.

VERONICA

88. Tim Mackie, *Themes: Holiness*, Jon Collins, BibleProject, accessed March 8, 2022, video, 00:06:35, https://bibleproject.com/explore/video/holiness.

89. "Purity and Impurity, Ritual," *Encyclopedia Judaica*, accessed March 9, 2022, https://www.encyclopedia.com/religion/encyclopedias-almanacs-transcripts-and-maps/purity-and-impurity-ritual.

90. See Leviticus 12:1–8, 15:19–30.

91. Fitzpatrick and Schumacher, *Worthy*, 93.

92. Reeder, *The Samaritan Woman's Story*, 120 and 123.

93. Fitzpatrick and Schumacher, *Worthy*, 95.

94. Fitzpatrick and Schumacher, *Worthy*, 95.

95. Reeder, *The Samaritan Woman's Story*, 120; John 9.

Endnotes

MARY MAGDALENE & THE RESURRECTION WITNESSES

Character portraits in this section owe to Justin Taylor ("Who Were the Women at the Empty Tomb?," *The Gospel Coalition: Between Two Worlds* (blog), April 11, 2014, https://www.thegospelcoalition.org/blogs/justin-taylor/women-empty-tomb) and the work of Richard Bauckham.

Although some early traditions collapse the identities of Mary Magdalene and Mary of Bethany, I chose to treat them as separate women because of the way they appear distinctly in the text.. Mary of Bethany is regularly discussed in reference to her sister Martha and brother Lazarus in the location of their hometown of Bethany, while Mary Magdalene is associated with a separate healing Jesus performed in Galilee. Mary Magdalene's prominence in the resurrection narrative is regularly connected to her well-known status among the early Christian church. If she and Mary of Bethany were the same person, the gospel writers would have no reason to use different names to distinguish them.

96.   Bauckham, *Gospel Women*, 212.

97.   Bauckham, *Gospel Women*, 119 and 134.

98.   Fitzpatrick and Schumacher, *Worthy*, 120.

99.   Bauckham, *Gospel Women*, 269–270.

100.   Bauckham, *Gospel Women*, 275.

101.   Bauckham, *Gospel Women*, 286.

102.   Bauckham, *Gospel Women*, 295.

103.   Luke 8:3

104.   Bauckham, *Gospel Women*, 35–36 and 110.

105.   Bauckham, *Gospel Women*, 150 and 161.

106.   A thorough argument for this connection is made by Richard Bauckham in *Gospel Women*, in his chapter titled "Joanna the Apostle" (109–202).

107.   Fitzpatrick and Schumacher, *Worthy*, 187.

108.   Reeder, *The Samaritan Woman's Story*, 173.

109.   Bauckham, *Gospel Women*, 59.

110.   Fitzpatrick and Schumacher, *Worthy*, 193.